RE-MEMBERING LIVES:
Conversations with the Dying and the Bereaved

by
Lorraine Hedtke
John Winslade

Death, Value and Meaning Series
Series Editor: John D. Morgan

Baywood Publishing Company, Inc.
AMITYVILLE, NEW YORK

Baywood Publishing Company, Inc.
26 Austin Avenue
Amityville, NY 11701
(800) 638-7819
E-mail: baywood@baywood.com
Web site: baywood.com

Library of Congress Catalog Number: 2003062951
ISBN: 0-89503-285-6 (cloth)

Library of Congress Cataloging-in-Publication Data

Hedtke, Lorraine, 1957-
   Re-membering lives : conversations with the dying and the bereaved / Lorraine Hedtke, John Winslade.
      p. cm. -- (Death, value, and meaning series)
   Includes bibliographical references (p.) and index.
   ISBN 0-89503-285-6 (cloth)
   1. Death--Psychological aspects. 2. Terminally ill--Psychology. 3.
Bereavement--Psychological aspects. 4. Grief. I. Title: Remembering lives. II. Winslade, John. III. Title. IV. Series.

BF789.D4H4 2004
155.9'37--dc22   2003062951

Table of Contents

Dedication

Re-membering Virginia, Maida, Julia, and Louise.

Keeping their stories alive opened us to new possibilities.

Preface

LORRAINE

From a young age, I have known death. Death of friends and family members as well as my own personal scrapes with unexpected events. It seemed, for better or worse, death was always around. When I made the decision to work with people who were dying and their families, it was a choice that made sense. I had, after all, been kissed by death often enough in my short life that I felt at home with this eventuality. This work was a kind of calling that offered comfort to me when I responded.

The professional milieu where I answered this calling has changed over the years. I have found myself working in medical hospitals and psychiatric settings, hospices, hospital emergency rooms, and private practice. In each of these domains, I have sought to develop some threads of constancy in my practice. My ardent desire has been to help people more fluidly and richly describe their lives, rather than flounder in or be suffocated by their problems.

Perhaps because of my personal brushes with death, or perhaps because of my professional involvement, I have been suspect of ideas that suggest that death is final. All too often, I witnessed deaths where emotional injury was layered on top of physical malady. Loved ones were routinely asked to "say good-bye" to a person who only minutes before an untimely happenstance had been full of vital life energy. Families made difficult life and death decisions flanked by labels ascribed to them by well-intentioned medical and mental health practitioners. Descriptions judging families who were in emotional turmoil as "in denial" or "avoidant" or worse, were commonplace in the dominant discourse of modernist medical conversation.

The dominant discourse was, thankfully, unsatisfying for my taste when I met people and tried to offer respectful assistance. I say thankfully, as it was this ongoing search that led me to the Institute for Creative Change in Phoenix, Arizona. My involvement began with the ICC just following graduate school. There, I had the good fortune to be exposed to a group of amazing thinkers who, like myself, were dissatisfied with mainstream therapeutic theory. I studied under the tutelage of Robert and Sharon Cottor, and explored postmodern thought, language theory, appreciative inquiry, discourse analysis, reflecting teams, social constructionism, and deconstructionism. With the Cottors, along with many other brilliant practitioners, I played with therapeutic theory and creative change practices. It is these practices, guided by this thinking, that I believe makes a difference in people's lives.

This scaffold was further constructed as I was exposed to the non-pathologizing language of narrative therapy. Based on many complementary postmodern frames of reference, narrative thought allowed my practice to flow and take shape in ways that were enlivening.

Over the past several years, I have had the good fortune to have John Winslade's encouragement. It was through conversations with him that I theorized more fully what I was already articulating in practice. John's keen thoughts sharpened my practice and persuaded me to bring pen to paper (or fingers to keyboard).

JOHN

Death and its friend grief have visited me on a number of occasions in my life too. The most notable occasion was the death of my daughter Julia at the age of five months some 22 years ago. It has remained for me a defining event. Other family members have died and not provided the same degree of challenge that Julia's death did. She has continued through the years to both live on in my memory and to feature in my life in sometimes surprising ways.

I always had a slightly uncomfortable relationship with conventional grief theory as a result of the experience of Julia's death. In my professional life, when I found myself in a counseling role with people struggling with their own grief experiences, I had no other tools at my disposal, but I was often left with a hollow feeling about offering these ideas in my work.

It was not until 1993, when I first read Michael White's article entitled "Saying Hullo Again" (White, 1989), that a penny dropped for me. It was as if a series of experiences and professional inklings quickly lined up to form a departure from what I had previously known. It was not a gradual change of perspective as I have experienced in other domains.

Since then, I have embraced a constructionist perspective in think-ing about grief in my personal life and in my professional counseling and teaching work. When my mother died in January 2001, I noticed how these ideas rendered the experience of her death richly life-affirming. Remembering her continues to be a subject of joy for me. This does not mean that I have no sense of loss and would not prefer that she were still alive. But grieving for her has on the whole not been very painful, even though it has been powerfully affecting.

In my teaching life, I continue to be struck by how easily people to whom I teach these ideas seem to latch onto them. Students and practitioners regularly seem to respond with, "Of course!," rather than with, "But. . . ." This response confirms my interest in the further development of these ideas and makes teaching them exhilarating.

When I met Lorraine, I was immediately drawn to her work in this domain and to a sense of like-mindedness. Very early on I introduced her to Julia and she responded with a warm interest that is not common. I have continued to enjoy listening to her stories of practice. Her work has touched me, stimulated my thinking and inspired me to reach further in this work. This book is populated with many stories from Lorraine's work and only a few from mine. Without the foundation of her experience, I could not have undertaken this project. But our writing is not just a direct report on practice either. We have spent many hours talking through the work that is represented here. These conversations have been crucial to the writing of this book.

LORRAINE AND JOHN

As we have been writing this book, we have imagined readers who are practitioners in a variety of disciplines who have in common their professional association with people who are dying and their families. We would include here those who work in the general psychological domain: mental health clinicians, family therapists, caseworkers, social workers, psychologists, counselors, and psychiatrists. We also hope that it has relevance for those who encounter death in medical settings, such as physicians and nurses. There are also many who work specifically with the dying and bereaved, such as clergy, hospice workers, bereavement counselors, funeral directors, and planners. And there are students who may find this work relevant to their course of study in psychology, gerontology, counseling, pastoral theology, thanatology, nursing, or social work.

Although the book is primarily aimed at a professional audience, we also believe that these ideas may hold personal interest. Death is not a subject that matters only in professional domains. Nor can we choose a life without death. Our hope is that readers from any walk of life may find ideas here that can open up possibilities in their relationship with death that they have not considered before. We do not see this as a morbid book about death but as a book of love stories, remarkable relationship tales, and inspirational practices.

We are grateful to many people whose stories of life and death are represented in these pages. Many of them are no longer alive in body but we are pleased to offer them a place to live on in written story. They have been generous in offering consent for their stories to be told in this medium. In an important sense, they have been authors alongside us in this project.

There are a number of other people who deserve acknowledgment for their contribution to the writing of this book. Cheryl White and David Denborough at Dulwich Centre Publications have offered Lorraine consistent encouragement in recent years through inviting her to showcase her work in conference presentations and in journal articles. This encouragement has spurred the further development of this writing into book form.

For Lorraine, the Institute for Creative Change in Phoenix deserves acknowledgment for being a significant part of her membership club. The refreshing thinking that takes place there has been a cool mist in the heat of the desert. For John, the community around the counseling program at the University of Waikato has been a similar source of ongoing stimulation. In particular, Wendy Drewery, Kathie Crocket, Wally McKenzie, and Gerald Monk deserve his appreciation. They have breathed warm academic life into frosty mornings on the banks of the Waikato River.

Angus Macfarlane deserves thanks and acknowledgment. Angus was helpful in confirming John's understandings of Maori perspectives on death and grief.

Our children deserve mention. They are our hope for being remembered ourselves. Lorraine is indebted to her daughter, Addison, for teaching her about inter-generational remembering. Addison has selflessly allowed Lorraine to tell the stories that connect Addison to her grandmother and her great-grandmother to audiences around the world. John's first child, Julia, has her own story to tell on some pages in this book and is present as a background witness on many other pages. His other children, Benjamin, Zane, and Joanna, are fine young members of the club of his life. When their grandmother died, they all enriched John's community of remembering in ways that reached beyond what they fully appreciate.

Lastly, and with the utmost reverence, we thank the many people who have shared their lives with us as they faced death. To their families who have carried their stories with grace, we are eternally grateful. We are proud to have these individuals as members in our club of life.

CHAPTER ONE

Why Remember?

Re-membered lives are moral documents and their function is salvific, inevitably implying, "All this has not been for nothing."
(Barbara Myerhoff, 1982, p. 111)

When I (Lorraine) met with Sebastian for the first time, we had an opportunity to plant seeds with his family about his hopes for their remembering of him. He had delightful ideas about how he envisaged his life continuing to be important to them following his death. With his wife, two children, his grandson, and two-month-old great-granddaughter, we spoke about his life. From his hospital bed, Sebastian shared how music had been so important to him and his family. He had been a music teacher and composer and each of his children also had a musical proclivity. They mentioned, almost in passing, that he was hoping to write music for the heavenly choir. I asked him about this. Was being in the choir an avocation that he would enjoy?

"Yes," he said, "but I do not want to be just in the choir, but in charge of it!"

His family laughed and explained that Sebastian preferred to run shows, rather than be a follower.

"He has written such wonderful music for so long that his friends know what a good musician he is. Many people are asking him to save a seat for them in the heavenly choir," his wife said.

His children spoke about how their father's musical abilities had inspired them. Sebastian seemed to be enjoying this conversation and was laughing and smiling with them as they remembered various concerts and how family outings were accompanied by music.

"What kind of music would you like to bring to the heavenly choir?" I asked.

Sebastian laughed, "Hopefully, the kind of music that makes you want to be there."

"Do you think the kind of music that you will create would be the kind that people might flock to?"

1

"Yes, I hope so. I would want people to use it to find their way to heaven."

I asked, "Would this be like a calling card? A card that is calling them over to heaven?"

"Yes. I will make the music so they can find the way."

Later, when speaking privately with Sebastian's children, I learned that their father was the first person they had known who was about to die. All their grandparents had died long before they were born. And, even though they were in their forties, they had had little death in their lives. They were having some trepidation about what death was like. They did not know what it would be like to grieve. Again, we spoke about their father's role with the heavenly choir. I wondered if they thought this was a fitting place for him. Did they think there was anything important about their father being the first to die in their family?

They spoke about how he had been their teacher throughout life and he was once again lighting the way for them. Their spiritual beliefs had always been a source of strength for them and they all shared a belief that afterlife meant heaven, in a Christian sense of the word. So for them to think of their father as in charge of the heavenly choir was apt.

"Some day, when it comes time for you too to die, what do you think it will be like to hear your father's music again?" I asked.

They liked the idea that he would welcome them back together after their deaths to sing as a family once more. They agreed that this was a reassuring thought.

> "It is comforting to know where my father will be, if I need him," his
> daughter said. "I like knowing that he will be content creating
> music and that it will be *his* music that will sing me over when *my*
> time comes to die."

STORIES HOLD MEANINGS

This story contains elements of the practices of professional conversation that we believe can make a difference for people when they are facing death in their families. It also prefigures some of the conversations that can help people negotiate the transitions that take place after a loved one has died. The central idea that we shall develop in this book is the idea of *remembering conversations;* that is, conversations in which a person's membership in relationship and family connections do not need be severed by the transitions that death brings (Hedtke, 2001a, 2001b, 2002b). When we think in terms of narrative continuity, we are free to construct conversations that are not bound by limited notions of "reality." In these conversations, we can invite out the ongoing significance of membership through the practice of remembering. Such conversations encourage people to bring forward the best possible experience of relationship in the face of the emergency of death. Even when we are faced with hardship, remembering gives us a clear path for making comforting meanings during confusing and challenging times. Sebastian's family was discussing how and where they would find their father and maintain a sense of relationship with him after his death. The trajectory that this conversation set in motion leads to ongoing opportunity for them to connect with the meaning of their father's life for years after his death. In a storied sense, this beginning allows them to remember him and keep him alive. Over the years, they might develop these stories to grow the connection through the process of remembering.

Sebastian, as he is dying, enjoys the comforting sense that he will live on in memory and story for his family and his friends. In our conversations, his family has the opportunity to reflect on what has been important in his life and how are they going to continue to honor their connection. This affords him the very important position of laying the ground work for how he will feature with his family in future. We are not leaving to chance the prospect of them remaining connected. Rather, we are asking Sebastian to remain in a directing role and to state what will be comforting to him as he takes up the challenges that death brings.

Through the course of the book, we shall elaborate on the specifics of the practice of remembering conversation in a variety of contexts. We shall look at the impact of remembering for the person who is dying as well as their loved ones. But first, here is another story by way of instructive example.

I (Lorraine) first met Josephina at her home just after the New Year. She had enrolled in hospice only a few days before, but was questioning if this was the right thing for her to do. She thought she might be premature in needing assistance to die. She and her two friends explained to me about the numerous radiation treatments and it became clear that the intractable pain she was suffering meant that Josephina could benefit from hospice care. Her face and voice were soft and she looked much younger than her fifty-six years. She told me that she had been diagnosed with colon cancer two years previously. Even after surgery, radiation, and chemotherapy, she remained upbeat and thought she could overcome cancer. It was not that she was afraid to die, she told me, it was just that her family needed her still. She was still trying to make sense of her doctors saying that there was nothing more that could be done.

Josephina had feared that things might be changing. She mentioned that she was having a harder time recalling details. The day before, she had fallen in the shower. She was now having a hard time supporting her own weight. Her friends had tried to stay with her as much as possible. They wanted to help and her husband was working and not often around.

"He is having a hard time with this," they said, when she was unable to hear them.

Her children were young adults with families of their own. Prior to being so ill, Josephina watched over her grandchildren while her son and daughter were working.

I reassured Josephina that being with hospice could help her. I was concerned, however, that she was in need of more assistance and that her friends and family might need to surround her differently. A few days later, we met again. When I arrived, her daughter was there with her four-year-old son and six-week-old daughter. The house was full of bustle and activity. People came and went and the children were in a noisy mood. This all fitted nicely with how Josephina's life had been when she used to teach kindergarten. She seemed to thrive on the activity and having her children and grandchildren around. Her daughter too was teaching elementary school.

I asked Mary, Josephina's daughter, about both of them being teachers. What did it mean to have this connection? Rather than asking about the anticipation of loss, I was seeking a conversation about its opposite.

Mary said she admired her mother and wanted to give to children as she had seen her mother do over the years.

"What do you think it means to your mother that you have followed in her footsteps?" I asked.

She replied that it would be important to always be as gentle as her mother has been. "She showed me how to be with kids—both in how she was to me and my brother and my own kids. She is the same with the kids she teaches too."

We spoke at length about how they would keep alive Josephina's stories and image for their grandchildren. In our view, remembering is very much a process of narrative construction. As we remember, we tell stories and the stories in turn embody and enliven our memories. Josephina and Mary were both concerned about how Mary's children, being so young, would remember their grandmother. We talked about how it might be to continue folding stories of their grandmother into the children's lives.

I asked Josephina which things she would like her grandchildren to know about her.

She said that she hoped they would know how nice she was and how much children meant to her. Mary had bought a book about stories from grandmothers. They spoke about filling in parts of it before she died as a project they could do together. It was important to Mary as well that the children come to know their grandmother as they grew.

CONTINUING MEMBERSHIP

Notice the focus of this conversation. It is not about delving into the emotions that might be produced in response to anticipatory loss. It is not about accepting the harsh reality of death. Nor is about producing closure or completing unfinished business. It is about relationship going on and it is about what might continue rather than what might be lost. We are proposing in this book that this is a more useful focus for conversations before and after death than a focus only on loss and pain. We shall explain along the way why we propose this to be a more useful focus, but suffice it to say at this point that our concern is not to magnify pain, and to imagine that this is the most helpful professional task. We prefer to magnify what might be comforting in the face of death.

The following week, I met with Josephina and Hector, her husband. Prior to this meeting, she told me that her husband "could be kind of difficult." She wanted her sister to come and stay with her and was concerned that her husband would not like that. They had never got along. She told him what she wanted and her concerns that they would fight. She told him peace was important to her as she knew she had very few days left and she wanted them to be peaceful. Hector spoke with surprising candor. He said he knew he had been a difficult husband. He said that for the first part of their marriage he had drunk too much and had yelled. Josephina agreed. They spoke about her mother who had lived with them at the end of her life. She apparently had not liked Hector and had made this publicly known. As they retold these stories, they both laughed.

"She could see through me," he said. "That old lady had my number! Things weren't always good between us."

Hector started to cry as he told Josephina how scared he was about the future. He said that he knew people sometimes did not like him but that everybody liked his wife. "She is always soft and kind. When we are together, they don't see so easily how I can be kind of rough."

"What do you think they will see when your wife is no longer physically here to offer her softness?"

"That is what bothers me—they might just see my roughness. I don't want that. I don't want my kids to stop visiting if Josephina is not here."

"If you were to bring her soft and kind voice alive for years to come, what would be different? Would your kids want to visit?"

"Yeah, they might. If I could do that."

"Well, how would you do that?"

"I'd have to remember that she never yelled. Even when she was most angry, she stayed calm. I would have to remember that she was able to be polite to everyone."

"When you are bringing her soft and kind voice alive after she has died, you won't be yelling and you'll be polite? What will happen when you do this?"

"That will be a good start, I think. To remember to be polite. My kids would want to come around then."

Our conversation continued to explore many details about what it might be like for Hector to keep Josephina's image and presence alive with him. I asked things like how he was going to incorporate her voice and her softness in the future after she was gone? What was he hoping that people would say he had gained from having this kind woman as his wife? All these questions were geared intentionally to keep her membership present in his life and with her family. Toward the end of this conversation, he mentioned that these concerns had been feeling urgent to him. He had been feeling almost panicky about them. He had been thinking that, if he lost his wife's softness, people would not care much for him. Hector was particularly concerned that he would estrange his children and grandchildren without the warmth and balance his wife had always provided.

CONSTRUCTIVE CONVERSATIONS

These are examples of some of the possibilities of a remembering conversation. Remembering conversations can start long before death, as they did above. But this kind of conversation can also take place after someone has died. It is clear, here, that Hector is aware that death will change things. In order for Josephina's voice to carry on, he will have to incorporate her voice more into himself and be responsible for carrying on its speaking. The professional conversation exemplified here is about assisting this transition to take place and rehearsing details about how this story might be performed in the future. We want to look at the particular places where he can practice "softness" and look to the effects of such action. Our intention is to maximize the beneficial implications of these steps for Hector and his family. We would say that this is a "constructive" conversation. That is, it is about constructing a deliberate future that continues to include Josephina. It is not about a focus on her loss from the world of the future. For Josephina to know something of this future before she dies is also of tremendous comfort for her. It has the potential to reduce the sense that death in some way erases the meaning of her life.

MEMBERSHIP

These stories introduce the idea of remembering. It relies on a concept of membership that needs some explanation at this point. We are using the metaphor of membership in the sense developed by Barbara Myerhoff (1978, 1982, 1986) and Michael White (1989) to refer to the club of significant others in a person's life. We are all born into such a club and along the way we add to, and sometimes subtract from, the membership list of this club. Immediate family members usually have a place of significance in this membership club, and we then add friends, colleagues, partners, and children.

A person's membership club serves as a major reference point for the construction of identity. In the relationships between a person and the other members of the club of his or her life, identity positions are offered and taken up and identifications are authenticated. From this perspective, identity is a by-product of multitudes of dialogues with others around us who validate us to be who we are (McNamee & Gergen, 1999). A membership club is constituted by the aggregation of reciprocal exchanges of such processes of authentication. This club forms a significant discursive community from which we draw to make sense of the events of life. Meanings are exchanged within this club. Hence, we can claim that the meaning of a person's life exists substantially within this club.

Membership of this club is not all of the same rank or status, however. Some members are granted privileged status. They can even be granted life memberships. Other members are more peripheral. Parents or caregivers usually have privileged status in the meaning system of a young child, for example. Some are granted elevated status by a person's choice of life partner or close friends. Others have a place of significance that is more locally specific or temporally limited. Nor is privileged status guaranteed for life. Estrangements happen and divorces, for example, often bring about a re-shaping of the membership of the club. Acts of abuse or abandonment can lead to the revoking of privileged membership status.

It is often assumed, within the modernist discourse of death, that death itself cancels membership. When people are expected to accept the finality and reality of death, this is often what is meant. People are asked to withdraw their investment in relationship with the deceased and to reinvest in other relationships (Worden, 1982/1991). The metaphor invokes an economy of relationship that invites us to treat people like stocks that we invest in (presumably for our own profit). When our relational investments are no longer yielding high returns, we are encouraged to cut our losses and move on. From our perspective, the idea that a relationship ends and that the bereaved need to cease to recognize a dead loved one as a member of their club of life is a mistake. It assumes too great an identification of personhood with corporeal existence and of relationship with simultaneous physical presence (Epston & White, 1992). A moment's reflection can tell us that even after their biological death, our loved ones continue to exist in our minds. We continue to hear echoes of their words and to tell their stories and to recall their influences on us. We continue to make meaning around their lives each time that we talk about them, just as we continue to live out their significance in our own living. Sometimes, we find ourselves talking to them and conjuring up their advice for our lives. When a new child is born, we may see their likenesses reproduced. We may even imagine their delight in family developments that they would have rejoiced in but never had a chance to see in their lifetime (Hedtke, 1999, 2000, 2001b).

In all these senses, we would argue that personhood continues to live on long after the body dies. It may take a narrative rather than a biological form, but its effects are nonetheless material. We can say that people continue to live in this form as long as they are remembered. Their membership of our club of life need not end with death. And if membership does not end, then we can continue to honor and have relationship with those who are in our membership club, even after they are dead.

REMEMBERING

This brings us to the concept of remembering. If we start from the notion of membership described above, then it is clear that conventional psychological approaches to "memory" are inadequate as a basis for remembering. Psychology's modernist focus on the discrete individual has constructed memory as privately owned and stored within the computer files of the mind. But it is important to note that alternative ideas of memory and of the process of remembering have been proposed (Madigan, 1997; Middleton & Edwards, 1990; Sampson, 1993). These constructionist perspectives suggest that memory is a much more socially distributed phenomenon. We remember things in the context of what is discursively selected for attention and we remember things dialogically in response to other's utterances that call forth particular memories. Thus, memory can be considered a much more conversational process than one that is placed solely under individual sovereignty.

Anthropologist Barbara Myerhoff (1982) calls remembering a special form of recollection. She describes it in this way:

> To signify this special type of recollection, the term "re-membering" may be used, calling attention to the reaggregation of members, the figures who belong to one's life story, one's own prior selves, as well as significant others who are part of the story. Re-membering, then, is a purposive, significant unification, quite different from the passive, continuous fragmentary flickerings of images and feelings that accompany other activities in the normal flow of consciousness (p. 111).

Her stress is on re-membering[1] as an active process of calling forth membership in a restorative way. It is a creative process that develops the life narrative of the living through a process of interaction with the dead. It does not take the time of death as a moment of finalization of the relational possibilities.

Remembering is more than reminiscing. Myerhoff's construction here positions the person doing the remembering as an active subject directing the process rather than as passively subjected to a stream of recalled images over which she or he has no control. What is remembered then is not just a pale representation of a previously vivid reality. It is an ongoing construction of a present reality. It is not so much a process of recalling past membership, so much as an invocation of current membership status.

Tom Attig's (2001) description of the role of memory in an ongoing relationship with a dead loved one captures something of the quality of living relationship that is possible.

---

[1] Barbara Myerhoff uses the word re-membering with a hyphen to emphasize the re-introduction of membership. That is our intention here too but we have decided to use the word remembering throughout this book without the hyphen in order to make the text easier to read. Because we are using this term so often throughout this book, we felt that it could start to look irratatingly pedantic to change the conventional spelling on every occasion.

> As we cherish memories, we return to freshen and deepen our understanding of those who died, attend to them again, bring them closer, embrace them in their absence, reconnect with some of the best in life, feel grateful, feel the warmth of our love for them, sense that they are grateful for our remembering, and feel the warmth of their love for us (p. 48).

Remembering in the sense that Attig is speaking of is a more active process than casual reminiscing. It produces in us, says Attig, a process of "relearning the world" (Attig, 1996).

Remembering conversations are deliberate acts of membership construction. They keep a person's membered status close and current and constantly renew our loved one's presence in our club of life. To remember is to include them in our daily lives, in our conversations, in our celebrations, in our decision making, and in our resources for living. To remember is to refuse to allow our loved one's memory to go by unnoticed. Remembering may involve keeping a person's voice alive through repeating their words in relation to new developments in life. It may involve consulting the deceased's opinion as a resource for dealing with a new challenge. It may involve keeping a place in family gatherings or rituals for someone who is no longer alive. It may involve telling young children stories about a dead grandparent's life. It may involve committing oneself to living for some value or purpose that a dead loved one held dear.

The use of the term "remembering conversations" is significant too. It suggests the importance of conversations in the construction of personal and social reality. This is the social constructionist perspective which we shall say more about later, that the meanings we construct in the significant conversations of our lives exercise a shaping effect on our experience (Gergen, 1994, 1999). Remembering conversations also build on Bakhtin's (1981, 1986) concept of dialogical thinking, in which ideas grow best in the fertile soil of conversational exchange.

For Myerhoff, the notion of remembering was developed to account for a social process of community renewal in the face of the death of a community member in a community of ageing Jewish people in Venice Beach in Los Angeles (Myerhoff, 1978, 1982, 1986). Remembering served a social and political process that the notion of loss would not have served. A political procession was organized around the memory of a community member who had been accidentally killed to consciously contest and deny the social invisibility of this community. Surviving community members drew attention to the life of their community, inscribed it in mural form in their community center, attracted outsiders to bear witness to their cause, and defined themselves in relation to it. As Myerhoff (1986) describes, "they came into being in their own terms" (p. 263) through this process of remembering.

The "Reclaiming our stories, reclaiming our lives" project (McLean, 1995) set up by the Aboriginal Health Council of South Australia and the Dulwich Centre in Adelaide also used the process of remembering in their work with an Aboriginal community around their experience of deaths in custody. In this project, a group of families who had all experienced the loss of a family member while in police custody gathered for a week of conversations about the effects of injustices in their lives, with a particular focus on the ways in which their family members had died. Participants reported that they were often "allowed to remember for the first time" (McLean, 1995, p. 17). In the process of these conversations, healing took place, injustice was named, and the dead were also remembered for who they were rather than simply as objects of injustice. The experience reported was not just one of personal grieving but of the reinvigoration of a community.

From these examples, we can see that the kind of remembering we are speaking of is not just of individual significance. It takes place in a dialogical context rather than intra-psychically. We are using the term dialogical here in the sense meant by Bakhtin (1981, 1986) referring to the ongoing energy generated from people's utterances to each other in an endless stream that is never finalized. Remembering is also political in intent, as well as in effect. Remembering strengthens both an individual's and a community's position in relation to powerful discourses at work in the construction of their lives. Barbara Wingard and Jane Lester (2001) give testimony to this in their stories of remembering family members from whom they had been separated by the colonizing practices that instituted the "stolen generation" of Aboriginal children in Australia. Barbara Wingard (2001) states this point powerfully in this way:

> Finding ways to bring people with us, those who are no longer living, can make a big difference in people's lives. When we reconnect with those we have lost, and the memories we have forgotten, then we become stronger. When we see ourselves through the loving eyes of those who have cared for us our lives are easier to live (p. 43).

Michael White (1997) is also concerned about the operation of power in the personal oppression of individuals when he stresses the possibilities for the person who is remembering taking charge of the re-allocation of membership status. He says:

This notion of remembering, and the club metaphor, suggests possibilities for persons to engage in a revision of the membership of their club of life. This is an engagement that provides persons with the opportunity to have a greater say about the status of particular memberships of their club of life. Through remembering practices, persons can suspend or elevate, revoke or privilege, and downgrade or upgrade specific memberships of their lives. Various classes of honorary membership can be established and bestowed, including life memberships. It is in this way that persons can have more to say about whose voices are to be recognized on matters of their identity, and about who might be authorized to speak on such matters (p. 23).

His concern here is for people to stand up to those who have imposed privileged membership in someone else's life and have then abused the privilege and done damage. The allocation of membership status in our lives is never totally a voluntary matter of individual choice. It is negotiated socially in the contexts in which we live. But neither is it impossible for individuals to exercise some agency especially in allocating the privileges that go with the subtler nuances of membership status. Even after death, it is possible to re-allocate such privileges and move people to more peripheral positions in the membership club and, therefore, limit their defining role in the ongoing process of identity construction. The same is true in reverse. After a person has died, their membership status can be revised in the light of developing life experience to value their contribution more.

DISMEMBERING

What is the opposite of remembering? The usual inclination would be to suggest forgetting. However, within the definition of membership that we are speaking about, this is too weak a term. If remembering keeps membership alive and continually activates and calls upon the privileges of such membership in our club of reference, then its opposite is not just a cognitive process. It amounts to the creating of a social division, one that separates people from relationships that are significant for them. In a sense, it tears people from each other's arms. We therefore prefer the term dismembering to describe the processes that separate people from their bonds with each other in the wake of death.

In the next chapter, we shall examine how some of the dominant medical and psychological models have supported practices that have had a dismembering effect. In doing so, we believe that these practices have rendered death and grief, at times, more painful than is necessary. In other words, we think it is possible to mount an argument that some of the pain that people experience as they negotiate bereavement is iatrogenically produced. We would therefore advocate an assessment of many of the ideas that dominate in the domain of death and grief that poses the question, "Does this idea or this practice promote remembering or dismembering of the dead?"

Let us list some examples of the ideas we are referring to that can promote dismembering. The idea that it is wrong or unhealthy to maintain a sense of attachment to someone who has died makes illegitimate a person's desire to do so. The greater the authority behind the voice that is speaking to this idea, the greater the de-legitimizing power of such an utterance. In the discourse of death and grief, this idea gets articulated as the encouragement to "let go" of the dead loved one. We may also be encouraged to "say good-bye" to the dead person and to accept the "reality" of the death in order to reach "closure" and "move on" from the loss. Each of these ideas works to build distance between us and our loved ones, rather than connection. For some people, this can even feel like cutting off a part of themselves. Hence, the term dismembering has a particular resonance that we find apt.

We are not the first to propose the use of the term "dismembering." Stephen Madigan used "dismembering" to describe the work being done by the discourse of anorexia to separate women from remembered identities that were being sidelined by anorexia's demands (Madigan, 1997). The context is different in that Madigan was not referring to practices of grieving after death, but the assumptions about the use of discourse to delegitimize connections and relationships in ways that have profound impact on a person's ongoing construction of identity are similar. The value placed on remembering as a practice where the social construction of identity in conversation takes place is also the same.

Ken Doka's description of the ways in which grief is "disenfranchised" in some contexts is also related to the way we are referring to "dismembering." Doka defines disenfranchised grief as "grief that is experienced when a loss cannot be openly acknowledged, socially sanctioned, or publicly mourned" (Doka, 2002, p. 160). He is referring to experiences of grief that are not recognized or not acknowledged, or fall outside of the category of socially sanctioned relationships that are considered primary (for example in relation to the deaths of unmarried lovers, pets, people over a hundred years old, neighbors, etc). There is overlap here with the idea of remembering that we are describing. Both refer to the silencing and distancing effects of social practices. However, we do not just want to re-enfranchise people's right to grieve. Rather we are focusing on the restoring of relationship and are critical of many of the dismembering effects of "grieving" for those whose grief is not disenfranchised under Doka's definition. We do not use the word "dismembering" lightly. We know the literal meaning to be sharp and shocking. We would argue that the act of removing a loved one from their community and their family could be similarly abrasive and shocking. We suspect that requirements on people to do this magnify pain and distress at a time when people are already experiencing the pain of loss.

However, we do need to acknowledge a danger in the use of this term. An incident illustrates this concern. Following a workshop, a woman quietly approached me (Lorraine) and mentioned that she had had a hard time hearing the word "dismemberment." The reason, she explained, was that her son had died following a tragic accident that had actually physically dismembered him. The word carried a particularly powerful resonance for her that we are not intending. To the contrary, in such circumstances we would not encourage the remembering of this moment of physical dismembering. In this particular conversation, we deconstructed some of the impact of the metaphorical resonance and discussed how it was important for her to keep her son's memory membered in her life and in their family. So, even in the context of a physical dismembering, remembering was of crucial value.

Although her example of dismemberment was dramatic, we believe that when people are invited to let go and move on, the effect does in fact violate a relationship. It is sometimes not unlike cutting off our own limbs. Another story speaks poignantly to this effect.

DELORES'S STORY

Delores and I (Lorraine) had often talked while her husband was alive. I loved visiting them, because I would always come away with the fullest love stories that uplifted me. I felt blessed to be sitting with these warm-hearted people. They had been married for more than fifty years when Delores' husband became ill. Throughout his illness, Delores provided the most devoted support. After his death, I was concerned about how Delores was going to adjust to the daily change in her time, as her care-giving efforts were no longer required. I would call her periodically, just to touch base. Many times when I phoned, she told me she was fine and, in fact, she thought she was doing much better than she had expected. One day when I phoned, Delores asked if we could talk. I arrived at her house to find that Delores was obviously distressed and had been crying. She soon relayed what had taken place.

As Christmas approached, she had been addressing Christmas cards and had run out of her pre-printed return address labels. She rummaged through her desk and found some old labels which had Delores's name and her husband's name printed upon them. Thinking that it might make people uncomfortable to receive a Christmas card from a dead man, Delores had taken out a pair of scissors and had begun to cut off her husband's name from the labels. As she was telling me this, she again began to cry and explained how it felt like she was cutting her beloved man out of her life.

This simple act was a powerful metaphor, one that I am always reminded of when I think about dismembering practices in relation to death. I wondered what informed Delores to act in this way. What might produce this belief that she should not have her husband's name on the Christmas labels anymore? How had she come to know that to cut his name off the cards was the socially acceptable thing to do?

This act of "cutting off" was emotionally painful for Delores, because it was an act of dismemberment, and she had been doing so well at remembering. Delores told me how wrong it felt to her to cut her husband out. It went against the grain to cut herself off from him. But Delores had felt constrained to act in this way in anticipation of what other people would think. This is a clear example of how a normalizing gaze (Foucault, 1978) can be internalized and influences the construction of relationship. Delores clearly experienced the effects of this construction as very painful. And yet she instinctively knew what might be said of her in the dominant discourse if she did not cut her husband's name off. Acts such as sending Christmas cards from a dead person run the risk of attracting pathologizing labels. The pain she was experiencing at this moment was not just the personal and individual pain of grief. It was the pain of being torn between her desire to remember and the pull of the dominant discourse that required dismembering.

*   *   *

We have now introduced the major ideas that this book will develop. We shall go on to develop them in different contexts of conversation. But before we do so, it is necessary to locate them in the context of the discourse of death and bereavement. That will be our task in the next chapter.

CHAPTER TWO
Death and Grief in the Modern World

> The grieving process is indeed embedded within cultural tradi-
> tions, and to approach the therapeutic or counseling setting with
> a universalist (and more specifically a modernist) preference for
> breaking bonds is not only to undermine existing patterns of cul-
> ture, but to throw into question normalcy or emotional adequacy
> of an otherwise unproblematic segment of the population.
>
> (Stroebe, Gergen, Gergen, & Stroebe, 1996, p. 40)*

How did death grow to have its present day meaning? We have not always understood death and grief as we do in the early 21st century. This chapter will look at some influences that have shaped the discourse of death in recent history. We are not attempting to write a full history of death but to point to some major assumptions built into the modern way of dying and the modern way of grieving. These assumptions can then serve as points of departure for exploring some alternative approaches to death.

This brief genealogical exploration will be built on the background idea that we are living in a world which is dominated by the modernist agenda. We take this to mean a particular approach to life that orig- inated in Western Europe and came to a position of dominance roughly at the time of the Enlightenment in the 17th century. Modernist think- ing has successfully colonized many other cultural traditions all around the world. This approach to life emphasizes the following assumptions as fundamental: "the unity of humanity, the individual as the creative force of society and history, the superiority of the west, the idea of science as Truth, and the belief on social progress" (Seidman, 1994).

Jean-Francois Lyotard (1984) referred to these assumptions as the dominant "meta-narratives" of the modern world.

We want to locate this book in the emergent world of post-modern thought, which is characterized by "incredulity towards meta-narratives" (Lyotard, 1984). Lyotard observed a decline in the legitimating authority of the foundational theories of knowledge and of social progress. Michel Foucault (1972, 1978, 1980) contributed to the decentering of these meta-narratives by pointing to the entangle-ment of knowledge and power in the production of modern life. He asked us to read the social sciences, not so much as places where human life was being objectively studied, but rather as places where it was actually being produced in the form of discourse. In other words, we should expect scientific knowledge to be shot through with cultural assumptions and to find that these assumptions are reproduced in many other domains of life, all of which are underpinned by discourse.

In the field of death and grief, then, we want to notice how the modernist agenda has been made manifest, the kinds of knowledge that the dominant meta-narratives of medicine and psychology have produced, and the cultural assumptions that have been privileged in the process. We are talking here about how dominant discourses of death can be found echoed both in academic theories and also in daily conversation. In particular, we want to question the following assumptions about death and grief:

- the unity of death and grief experiences across different cultural contexts
- the place of the individual at the center of the psychology of grief
- the assumption of death as a psychological finality because it repre-sents a biological finality
- the expectation that grief will be a heavy and sad process which culminates in the individual successfully detaching from a relation-ship with the deceased
- the implicit requirements in many theories of grief for people to produce themselves in ways that fit into a world dominated by a modernist agenda.

Modern ideas about death are even under threat in their own terms. Robert Neimeyer has pointed out that scientific studies have generally failed to support the existence of emotional stages that people pass through as they adapt to loss. They have also not been able to identify any discernible endpoint that would count as "recovery" from a grief experience (Neimeyer, 2001). Nor has "grief work" that amounts to dwelling on what is lost been found to produce positive psychological benefits (Stroebe & Schut, 2001).

There is too a growing literature about death and grief that questions the modernist assumptions. In this literature, the following aspects of modernist thinking have come into question:

- the goal of detachment or disengagement from the dead as the endpoint of grieving (Attig, 2000; Klass, 2001; Neimeyer, 2001; Silverman & Klass, 1996; Stroebe, Gergen, Gergen, & Stroebe, 1996)
- the idea that grief can be definitively resolved or that closure is a desired goal (Rosenblatt, 1996; Silverman & Nickman, 1996; Stroebe, Gergen et al., 1996)
- the individualistic emphasis on striving for independence in grief resolution rather than for relationship (Hagman, 2001; Neimeyer, 2001; Silverman & Klass, 1996; Stroebe, Gergen et al., 1996)
- the conception of grief as like an illness that moves from equilibrium to disequilibrium and back to equilibrium again (Neimeyer, 2001; Silverman & Klass, 1996)
- the over-emphasis on grief as a passive emotional experience to the exclusion of cognitive and behavioral dimensions (Neimeyer, 2001; Silverman & Klass, 1996; Worden, 1982/1991)
- the uniform or universal applications of grief theory without regard for cultural context (Klass, 1996; Neimeyer, 2001; Rosenblatt, 1996; Stroebe, Gergen et al., 1996).

However, our main reason for questioning these assumptions is that we believe that the postmodern stance of "incredulity" toward the dominance of these ideas might release us to open up new possibilities for dying and grieving. What might happen, we are asking, if we assume that the meaning of death is a product of culture and discourse? How might we talk with people without urging them to view death as final in terms of relationship and, therefore, requiring the completion of unfinished business and the performance of good-bye rituals? What differences might we notice if we focused more on relational than on individual dimensions of death? And what might happen if we questioned some of the parameters of modern life rather than invited the production of grief to fit tidily within its conventions?

THE DISCOURSES OF DEATH
IN MODERN LIFE

Rather than attempt to outline an exhaustive account of death and grief in modern life, we want to take a snapshot approach in this section. We shall examine a series of pieces of text from academic and from lay sources that can be taken to represent some of the major discourses at work in the construction of the dominant cultural ideas about death and grief.

MEDICAL DISCOURSE

The first piece of text comes from a medical chart. It represents the way in which a person's life and imminent death is constructed in everyday medical discourse in the modern world.

> 87 y.o. cauc. ♂ with ES Lung CA: Stage IV. Mets to Bone. CC:SOB.
> 3-6 month prognosis. Full Code.

Let us notice how personhood and relationship with death is being constructed in this piece of text. The person brought into being here is focused upon in a certain limited way. Biological existence (for example, stage IV lung cancer) is being privileged over family, social, or spiritual life, and symptoms (such as shortness of breath) over personal meanings or experience. The person has become a patient who is spoken of like many other patients in "objective" language. We can notice how membership is referenced to race and gender only (he is a Caucasian male) rather than to other aspects of cultural identification. Race defined by skin color and gender are major aspects of social division in the modern world. The patient is constructed primarily in individual terms rather than as a member of a family or a community.

The fact that the person is ill or dying is scarcely acknowledged. Indeed the mention of "full code" suggests that the medical staff will work intensively against the enemy of death until the last possible minute. They may do this in response to the legal discourse that dominates the context in which they work, rather than in response to any preferences of the person concerned.

The "full code" status may also indicate a yardstick in the medical arena against which to measure a person's individual acceptance. In spite of discourse inviting a person to continue to fight their illness, assumptions are made that if "the patient" with a terminal diagnosis/prognosis (or their family members) persist in wanting treatment of "aggressive or heroic measures", then they are not accepting of death. It may even be said that they are living "in denial." Each of these phrases carries weight and meaning within medical settings and can objectify persons into identities.

This piece of text reminds us of the extent to which modern death has been constructed as a medical event taking place in a hospital. Often, it even represents a failure of medical intervention to prolong life. It is worth remembering, though, that this is historically a recent development. Prior to the mid-20th century, death remained an event that usually took place in people's homes. Like birth, death was an integral part of ordinary life. The medical world was frequently left out (Aries, 1974; Bertman, 1997; Silverman & Klass, 1996).

Since then, however, death has become increasingly medicalized and medical discourse has gained greater influence over our experience of death. The body has come to be diagnosed, treated, and dissected in a modular way through the evaluation of its parts. Disease has become the enemy and death the ultimate defeat. The military metaphor is apt, because there was a link between 20th century warfare and the growth of hospitals (Benoliel, 1997). After World War I, there was a marked increase in the number of hospitals and the medicalization of dying accelerated. Aries (1974) also makes the link between these developments explicit:

> Between 1930 and 1950 the evolution accelerated markedly. This was due to an important physical phenomenon: the displacement of the site of death. One no longer died at home in the bosom of one's family, but in the hospital, alone (p. 87).

Death, and birth, were taken out of the home and became hospital events, where previously people had been tended to by family and friends when they became ill. The family doctor may have paid a visit but offered little in the way of surgery or extensive drug intervention. Medical knowledge at the time was couched in a vocabulary that was easier for lay people to understand than the complex terms and procedures used now, which can often only be understood by people in the medical professions.

However, the balance of knowledge/power has shifted in favor of the physician and away from the family and the community. On the basis of the modernist belief in the inevitability of social progress, new treatments are developed to prolong life, sometimes at the cost of quality of life, particularly if measured in terms of family relationships.

SIGMUND FREUD AND
PSYCHOLOGICAL DISCOURSE

The next piece of text we shall include comes from Freud (1917/ 1958) and is often cited for its influence on thinking about death and grief in the century since his death.

> Now in what consists the work which mourning performs? The testing of reality, having shown that the loved object no longer exists, requires forthwith that the libido shall be withdrawn from its attachment to the object. Against this demand a struggle of course arises—it may be universally observed that man never

willingly abandons a libido-position, not even when a substitute is beckoning to him. . . . The normal outcome is that deference for reality gains the day. Nevertheless its behest cannot at once be obeyed. The task is carried through bit by bit, under great expense of time and cathectic energy, while all the time the existence of the lost object is continued in the mind. Each single one of the memories and hopes which bound the libido to the object is brought up and hyper-cathected, and the detachment of the libido from it is accomplished. . . . When the work of mourning is completed the ego becomes free and uninhibited again (pp. 244-245).

And again from Freud (1938):

Grief is a prototype and perfect example of an affective fixation upon something that is past, and, like the neuroses, it also involves a state of complete alienation from the present and the future (p. 244).

These pieces of text represent the dominant psychological discourse of grief to this day. The voice speaking here is that of the authoritative scientist, making pronouncements of "universal" truth across all contexts and cultural difference about an objectified human subject. The person constructed in this discourse may be described as the modern rational man, grounded in reality and in the present, without a strong interest in the past. *He* (sic) is also not referenced to any cultural context in any noticeable way. When grief intrudes, he performs acts of decathexis in order to restore a normal relationship with reality. The struggle that he engages in is with the natural drive of his libido, which he gradually brings under control in order to make his contribution to society. There is no sense that this struggle may include the need to surmount obstacles set in place by the power relations in his world.

Grief, in Freud's texts, is constructed as a temporary abnormality, like an illness. Its energy is dissipated through the process of decathexis, that is, through emotional release. The pathway out of the "illness" of grief is based upon detachment from the "lost object." Successful grief is measured by the responses and coping ability of persons and by how well they readjust to life after a death. By contrast, the process of remembering is pathologized as a "fixation," not unlike a neurosis. It is hardly encouraged.

These basic assumptions have been elaborated in much of the literature on death and grief since Freud. They have been evident not only in the psychoanalytic and object relations literature, but also in humanistic approaches to grief. The signs and symptoms of grief have been prescribed and interpreted as universally valid, with little consideration for cultural and familial distinctiveness (Hagman, 2001;

Neimeyer, 2001). The psychology of grief has paid little attention to sociological or anthropological perspectives.

Conversely, remaining attached to the dead through thinking about them, talking about them, dwelling on them, or speaking with them has been constructed as abnormal or deviant (Silverman & Klass, 1996). Ongoing expressions of grief tend to be constructed as emotionally indulgent, or as taking people away from culturally preferred rational ways of being which are "required" in order to successfully contribute to society (Stroebe, Gergen, Gergen, & Stroebe, 1996). Such grief may be described as "unresolved."

John Bowlby's (1969/1980) developmental theory of attachment also lent weight to the ideal of detachment in the wake of death. Bowlby studied how children form attachments to their mothers and other caregivers, and posited a relationship continuum along an axis of attachment and separation. When these polarities are balanced, separation anxiety is decreased. When there is too much separation, the desire to restore attachment increases for most people. During the course of development then, according to Bowlby, we must successfully detach ourselves and live free from debilitating anxiety. However, the particular balance of attachment and detachment that was valued in Bowlby's theory as the desired goal of psychological adjustment may be deconstructed as a culturally bound assumption. Different cultures value attachment and detachment in different ways. Bowlby's resolution of this balance does not deserve to be credited with universal relevance. It appears to privilege a typically Western individualistic placing of high value on detachment. If this culturally specific goal of achieving sufficient detachment from loved others is valued when they are alive, then we should not be surprised if it was accorded even greater significance after death. But we also should not be surprised if an emphasis that leans toward detachment from loved ones does not work so well for many people.

The goal of helping people achieve an optimum degree of detachment (perhaps described as autonomy or self-responsibility) has been taken up as the task for therapy; that is, to assist people to form appropriate bonds and to effectively manage the loss of those bonds when the time comes. Grief therapy, therefore, has been constructed to assist the bereaved to heal through accepting the loss and restoring the autonomous self. Within this frame of thinking, the valued goal of detached individual status is not assisted by processes of remembering that emphasize how we continue to be entwined with the dead in an ongoing way. Remembering conversations, therefore, constitute a counter-story to the story of detachment as a goal of grief therapy.

ELISABETH KÜBLER-ROSS AND
DEATH AWARENESS

The third piece of text we shall consider is drawn from the writing of Elisabeth Kübler-Ross. Since the 1970s, her work has loomed large in the field of death and bereavement. Even a snapshot approach would not be complete without reference to this work. Kübler-Ross developed a description of the process of stages that dying patients in a Genevan cancer ward went through and then extended this work to include family members of the dying. Here is a sample extract from her book *On Death and Dying* (1969 edition).

> No matter what the underlying reason we should try to under-stand their (the dying person's family's) needs and to help relatives direct these needs constructively to diminish guilt, shame, or fear of retribution. The most meaningful help we can give any relative, child or adult, is to share his (sic) feelings before the event of death and to allow him (sic) to work through his feelings, whether they are rational or irrational.
>
> If we tolerate their anger, whether it is directed at us, at the deceased, or at God, we are helping them take a great step towards acceptance without guilt. If we blame them for daring to ventilate such socially poorly tolerated thoughts, we are blameworthy for prolonging their grief, shame, and guilt which often results in physical and emotional ill-health (p. 867).*

Kübler-Ross's efforts were directed at humanizing the more imper-sonal aspects of death under the medical regime. The psychology she draws from is still largely psychodynamic, but contains more humanistic emphases. It constructs the self primarily in terms of essential feelings that need to be "worked through" by sharing them with others. The distinction rational/irrational is drawn around such feelings and the preference is for the production of a rational self. The family context is invoked in this text but its members are constructed largely as individuals.

Freud's repression hypothesis lies in the background of this text and psychological health is assumed to be produced by the "con-structive" expression of emotion. And the chief job of those around the dying person is not to interfere with, or repress, such expression. Grief is thought of in terms of a natural progression through grief (shock, denial, anger, bargaining, and acceptance). These stages (and their elaborations by subsequent authors who built on her work) have enjoyed so much popular circulation that many lay people incorporate them in their assessments of their own and their family members' grieving.

The cultural environment around the person can best serve the requirements of healthy psychological development by giving the individual as much freedom as possible to express the essence of their experience. Kübler-Ross was critical of the dominant cultural context for its silencing of talk about death. To this extent she was interested in a deconstruction of the dominant cultural norms of her day. However, the psychological ideas that she drew on came straight from the mainstream of that cultural world. In her worldview, cultural difference is not constructed at the heart of the self, but around the psychological periphery with a largely negative role of interfering with nature. She assumed that people have a natural need to talk about death and grief. Given permission to do so, they would find a healthy developmental path. Absent from this analysis is the idea that the talk that people undertake might be constituted within the dominant discursive influences of their social world.

Kübler-Ross's work does include a brief reference to the incipient possibilities of remembering (1969). She writes:

> The last reason perhaps for patients' good response (*to requests to participate in her interviews*) is the need of the dying person to leave something behind, to give a little gift, to create an illusion of immortality perhaps . . . we tell them that their role is to *teach* us, to help those who follow them later on, thus creating an idea that something will live on after their death, an idea, a seminar in which their suggestions, their fantasies, their thoughts continue to live, to be discussed, become immortal in a little way (p. 262).*

The remembering referred to here is limited, however, to the context of the research seminar that Kübler-Ross had started. The patients would live on in the discussions that took place there. There was no effort to utilize this idea for the benefit of the dying patients or their family members. The pull of modernist scientific realism is also worth noting in passing in the use of the word "illusion" when referring to what might live on after death. "Reality" still remains firmly in charge. Kübler-Ross's preferences against remembering practices (1969) are made more explicit in the following piece of text:

Many relatives are pre-occupied by memories and ruminate in fantasies, often even talk to the deceased as if he was still alive. They not only isolate themselves from the living but make it harder for themselves to face the reality of the person's death. For some, however, this is the only way they can cope with the loss, and it would be cruel indeed to ridicule them or to confront them daily with the unacceptable reality. It would be more helpful to understand this need and to help them separate themselves by taking them out of their isolation gradually (p. 184).*

Here remembering practices are tolerated and "understood," rather than encouraged. This view is conveyed in the tone of words like "preoccupied," "ruminate," and "fantasies." Remembering practices are appreciated as slightly pathetic (if not pathological) responses which are not helpful in advancing the cause of grief resolution, the goal of which is facing the "unacceptable reality." The requirement that is constructed here seems to be that the grieving family member should make a choice between being isolated from the dead (that is, dismembered) or isolated from the world of the living. Such a forced choice does not seem necessary from our point of view.

WILLIAM WORDEN AND GRIEF THERAPY

The fourth snapshot we shall look at in this potted survey is of a piece of text from William Worden's book *Grief Counseling and Therapy*. Worden's contribution to this field has been in the development of a therapeutic approach for professionals who work with the bereaved. The two editions of his book on grief therapy (1982, 1991) provide a roadmap for counselors who help people negotiate the experience of grief. From our perspective, such roadmaps serve not only as objective descriptions of the topography of grief, but also as cultural products that give form and shape to the experience of grief itself. To some degree, all descriptions do more than describe. They become pieces of knowledge that impact on the discourse that they describe. Since Worden's work has been influential for therapists, we need to ask questions about what kind of personhood, what kinds of relationships, and what kinds of communities it envisions. We might also ask what traces of modernist assumptions can be found at work in the construction of his thinking.

One of Worden's concerns is to construct grief less as a passive experience that people suffer through, and more as an active process that people do. It is not just a matter of letting time heal, as of doing things, in time, to process losses. In this sense, he constructs the grieving person more as an agent in the shaping of her or his own life, and less as a patient who must wait out the period in which grief takes over and has its own way. This emphasis makes grieving less biologically "natural" in emphasis and more socially meaningful. It is something that people do, rather than something nature does to people.

Worden specifies four main tasks of mourning that the bereaved should work through (Worden, 1991). These four tasks deserve mention.

Task 1: To accept the reality of the loss
The first task of grieving is to come full face with the reality that the person is dead, that the person is gone and will not return. Part of the acceptance of reality is to come to the belief that reunion is impossible, at least in this life . . . (pp. 10-11).

Task II: To work through to the pain of grief
. . . It is necessary to acknowledge and work through this pain or it will manifest itself through some symptoms or other form of aberrant behavior . . . (p. 13).

Task III: To adjust to an environment in which the deceased is missing . . . (p. 14).

Task IV: To emotionally relocate the deceased and move on with life . . . (p. 16).
The counselor's task then becomes not to help the bereaved give up their relationship with the deceased, but to help them find an appropriate place for the dead in their emotional lives—a place that will enable them to go on living effectively in the world (p. 17).*

The empirical realism of modernist science is evident here. Reality is singular and self-evident and must be faced. From a postmodern perspective, however, there are alternative perspectives on reality. For example, reality might be considered as a product of the assumptions that we build into our view of it. It is something that we construct, rather than something that just is. We mediate its production through the cultural stories that we know. Hence, Worden's task of facing and accepting the reality of the loss is not so simple if we consider that we are creating what we are facing, even as we are adjusting to it.

*Reprinted with permission from Springer Publishing Company.

Worden's tasks are also presented as universally relevant across a range of cultural and social dimensions. Is it possible that all cultural contexts might require the same tasks? We would suggest that different types of death and different social circumstances and different cultural meanings of death and bereavement might radically alter the tasks that people who are grieving might commit to. If this is the case, then the description of a series of universal tasks risks obscuring and colonizing cultural differences under the modernist scientific banner.

The personal identity development that is privileged in Worden's model is in the direction of adjustment to the modern world, and living "effectively" in it. To do so, one must eventually "move on" from the grief. Failure to move forward, or to complete the tasks successfully, runs the risk of being described in terms of "symptoms of aberrant behavior."

Worden (1991) continues to specify the goals of grief counseling in relation to these required tasks of grieving. He states:

> The overall goal of grief counseling is to help the survivor complete any unfinished business with the deceased and to be able to say a final good-bye. There are specific goals and these correspond to the four tasks of grieving. These specific goals are:
> 1. To increase the reality of the loss.
> 2. To help the counselee deal with both expressed and latent affect.
> 3. To help the counselee overcome the various impediments to readjustment after the loss.
> 4. To encourage the counselee to say an appropriate good-bye and to feel comfortable reinvesting back into life (p. 38).

The saying good-bye metaphor is used explicitly here. It is an example of a notion in the discourse of grief that has gained widespread currency. The assumptions that underlie it, however, are still those that were present in Freud's emphasis on detachment and decathexis from the deceased.

In order to say such a good-bye, Worden suggests that "unfinished business" needs to be completed. The commercial metaphor is echoed again in the goal of "reinvesting" into life, connoting a modeling of relationship on the world of business transactions in which the flow of funds through a series of deals is the norm. Modern capitalism requires people to produce themselves as economic units in the form of consumers, workers, and investors. It encourages us (through such discourse) to conceive of relationships in similar ways, as deals done for profit, from which we withdraw capital when no more profit is to be made. If our goal is maintaining ongoing membership, however, rather than detaching and moving on, then there does not seem to be any rush to complete unfinished business ahead of saying good-bye. It might be more appropriate to discuss ongoing business in the context of ongoing relationship.

Another feature of this text is the construction of a relationship with self that is suggested in a phrase like "dealing with expressed and latent affect." The invitation, it sounds like, is to bring the emotional world under rational control. The distinction between "latent" and "expressed" invokes the psychodynamic mechanisms of cathected emotion dissipating through processes of decathexis. One might ask who is the self who is doing this work? Worden gives the impression that it is again the individual modern subject, the stable and rational citizen, of indeterminate cultural location, who is spoken into existence in such texts.

So what does Worden say that links with the idea of remembering conversation? In his 1991 revision he has actually made some movement in the direction of acknowledging the value of remembering. Rather than talking about "withdrawing emotional energy from the deceased," he moved to a statement about "relocating the deceased," (Worden, 1991, p. 16). He acknowledges that the bereaved often "never lose memories of a significant relationship" (p. 16) and defines relocating the deceased as evolving "some ongoing relationship with the thoughts and memories that they associate with [the dead]" (p. 17). Although Worden seems to be making a shift in language that has been noticed in professional literature (Neimeyer, 2001; Vickio, 1999), his change does not appear to be supported in the rest of the text. The grieving tasks that he continues to recommend contain assumptions that have not fully incorporated the implications of this shift of terminology.

THE DSMIV AND PSYCHOLOGICAL ASSESSMENT

The next piece of text is drawn from the American Psychiatric Association's Diagnostic and Statistical Manual (fourth edition). This document is highly influential in the mental health field in the United States and in many other countries. It is consulted by psychiatric and psychological professionals in the process of making diagnostic decisions and serves a powerful shaping influence in the construction of responses to the ways in which people present themselves to clinicians. It can be said to speak through many therapists' work and has become a benchmark requirement for financial reimbursement in third party (public and private insurance) payments. It is therefore worth noticing what the DSMIV says about grief.

V62.82 Bereavement

This category can be used when the focus of clinical attention is a reaction to the death of a loved one. As part of the reaction to the loss, some grieving individuals present with symptoms characteristic of a Major Depressive Episode (e.g., feelings of sadness and associated symptoms such as insomnia, poor appetite and weight loss). The bereaved individual typically regards the depressed mood as "normal" although the person may seek professional help for relief of associated symptoms such as insomnia or anorexia. The duration and expression of "normal" bereavement vary considerably among different cultural groups. The diagnosis of Major Depressive Disorder is generally not given unless the symptoms are still present two months after the loss. However the presence of certain symptoms that are not characteristic of a "normal" grief reaction may be helpful in differentiating bereavement from a Major Depressive Episode. These include 1) guilt about things other than actions taken or not taken by the survivor at the time of death; 2) thoughts of death other than the survivor feeling that he or she would be better off dead or should have died with the deceased person; 3) morbid preoccupation with worthlessness; 4) marked psychomotor retardation; 5) prolonged or marked functional impairment; 6) hallucinatory experiences other than thinking that he or she hears the voice of, or transiently sees the image of the deceased person (pp. 740-741).*

In this piece of text, the clinician is constructed principally in an assessment relation with the person being described. The assessment being made is about how normal the symptoms of grief are. They are to be assessed objectively from the outside rather than from any subjective standpoint and the criteria for the assessment are being specified. It is hard to see how a professional focusing on this diagnostic role could at the same time be focused on facilitating a remembering conversation.

Notice, too, the two month time frame that is specified for the "symptoms" of normal grief before other diagnoses such as depressive disorder, anorexia, or insomnia enter the field of analysis. When people are expected to move on and return to normal after a death, this is one influential specification of the length of time they might be given to do so. Some recognition is granted for cultural difference but the dominant focus is still on the individual internal functioning which is largely disconnected from any social context.

What happens to personal experiences of grief under such a regime? They are likely to be objectified and treated as "symptoms" of an

*Reprinted with permission from the *Diagnostic and Statistical Manual of Mental Disorders, Fourth Edition.* Copyright 1994 American Psychiatric Association.

underlying truth, rather than taken at face value. They are measured against an established standard (itself a cultural product although its cultural origins remain hidden) and the sword of pathology is raised ready to fall on any who stray too far from the norm. Grief is also constructed here as a largely negative, problematic experience which needs to be endured. There is little expectation of the experience of positive outcomes. The joys and satisfactions of remembering scarcely seem noteworthy.

THE HOSPICE MOVEMENT

The next piece of text comes from a leaflet published by the National Hospice Organization in the United States. It is included in recognition of the significant role played by the hospice movement in mediating experiences of death and bereavement in modern life. According to international statistics collected by St. Christopher's Hospice in London, there were an estimated 6,800 hospices and palliative care units world wide in 2001. These home and hospital based programs spanned 93 countries (St. Christopher's Web site, February, 2002). The National Hospice Organization now recognizes over 3,100 hospices throughout the United States (National Hospice Organization Web site, February 2002). These hospices served 540,000 people in 1998 and of these approximately 77% died in their own home. These numbers have more than doubled since 1992 and almost quadrupled since 1985 (Lattanzi-Licht & Connor, 1995; National Hospice Organization Web site, November 10, 1999).

Hospices, and the discourse of palliative care, began (originally in Britain in the 1960s) in order to offer an alternative approach to death from that which pertained in the dominant medical regime. Dame Cicely Saunders (1963, 2001) was a spokesperson for the early days of this movement who showed the world how it was possible to midwife death with appropriate pain medications (such as Brompton's mixture and various opiates) and psycho-spiritual support. Her visit to the United States in 1963 (Saunders, 2001) was influential in establishing the hospice movement there.

What developed in the hospice context was a concept of the peaceful death. This contrasted within the dominant medical idea of death as the enemy to be fought to the end. The hospice movement shifted the emphasis onto a consideration of the quality of the experience, rather than simply of the final outcome.

The brochure from which this text is taken is entitled *About Grief* (1997). It is produced for members of the general public whose loved one has died and is handed out by hospice workers to bereaved family members to help them make sense of their grief. The text is accompanied with simple cartoon drawings and is attractively laid out. We shall select for analysis some sentences of text from different parts of this brochure.

> What is grief? It is a natural reaction to any important change or loss. Grief is a healthy human response to situations such as the death of a loved one . . .
>
> Grief is a painful experience but the pain does subside.
>
> Understanding grief can help you: face the reality and deal with feelings of fear, loneliness, despair and helplessness; recover and grow to be a stronger person. Accepting your loss can help you live a happy life again.
>
> Living with loss. Take care of your emotional needs: express your feelings. Holding painful feelings inside can create more problems.

The speaker here adopts the tone of a friendly expert giving direct advice and basic information to a grieving person who is addressed in the second person. The apparent aim is to validate a range of personal experiences as "normal," and to encourage people to do certain things in response to their grief. Along the way, a series of assumptions get built in. While these assumptions are couched in the midst of descriptions, they can be expected to work as prescriptions too, guiding readers in how to shape their experience to fit the norm. It is worth noting that grief is constructed here primarily again in biological terms as a "natural reaction." There is no suggestion that our grief responses may be products of socio-cultural discourse or that the speaker is located in any social position. Grief thus appears something to be suffered through, rather than actively constructed. It is also described primarily as an experience of the emotions, which should be expressed for good health, if necessary with the help of a counselor. The mention that is made of cognitive shifts is the suggestion that understanding grief helps "face the reality" and "deal with" the emotions. Here we catch a glimpse of the modernist ideal—the rational, stable individual self, mastering emotions and standing tall to face down a unified, objectively valid "reality." The experience of grief appears to be an individual psychological one rather than a relational or communal event, and the socio-cultural context of the speaker and the person addressed are not made visible.

The leaflet goes on to give advice about what the individual griever should do to produce themselves as normal citizens again after the interruption of grief.

Set goals and work to reach them.

Try new activities. Join a club or organization. Take a new course.
Do some volunteer work. Evaluate your career goals.

You can live life to the fullest once again!

Counselors help people understand their feelings, create new goals
and adjust to their loss.

These utterances are offered as imperative constructions from
the position of professional expert, although in the sentence about
seeking help from a counselor, the tone is softened and the injunction
is more indirect. But the message is still clear, that if you are having
difficulty "adjusting to the loss," you should seek professional help.
Despite the concerns of hospice to establish a position of cultural
difference in relation to the medical discourse, the general discourse
of grief in the modernist social world is still maintained. Grief, like
illness, is a problem to overcome. Problem-solving activities are suggested. Moving on appears to be the goal. And no mention is made
of ongoing relationship with the dead person. In fact, the deceased
is noticeably absent from this text. The griever is invited to submit
to the expert professional advice and to enter primarily into a relationship with themselves as grieving persons, rather than with their dead
loved one. In other words, the effect of such discourse is again likely
to be dismembering (see Chapter One).

The Sympathy Card

Finally in this chapter let us turn to an aspect of popular culture—
the greeting card industry. Discourse theory (Burr, 1995) would suggest
to us that the same underlying assumptions of modernism that
drive academic knowledge might pertain to the domains of popular
culture, even though they get expressed in different genres. So let
us examine the text of a greeting card that might be given to someone after his or her loved one has died. For copyright reasons, we
cannot reproduce the text of one card. We have, however, constructed
a typical message by paraphrasing messages from several actual
cards to produce a simulated message. The text of this imaginary
card might, of course, be enhanced with floral pictures, embossed
words, and an attractive layout. But we can still regard the
words written on the card as emblematic of the discourse of death
and grief, as it gets expressed in sympathy cards. Here is the text of
such a card:

It's OK to grieve . . . and to think why me?
You may need to be alone . . . .
You may feel confused, and doubt you'll ever feel the same again.
Take all the time you need to get over this sadness.
In the end, precious memories will wipe away your tears.

What assumptions about death and grief, and about our relationships with each other in the midst of grief, are being reproduced here? First let us notice the voice that is speaking. It is one of reassurance and advice-giving from a position of knowing best. It gives permission for certain responses to death and omits other possible responses. Hence, the responses that it gives permission for are made socially legitimate while other possible responses are left in question.

What is legitimated seems to be the experience of death that features sadness and pain. The assumption seems to be of an individual experience, rather than a communal one ("you may need to be alone"). It is primarily an experience of the emotions, and the way through this experience is to intensify the feeling of the loss. The role of the person at the center of the grief seems to be constructed in a somewhat passive, suffering role. There is no sense of agency, as in Worden's tasks, nor of taking up the active role of remembering. The writer humanely gives permission to take time to grieve but the expectation is there that this time will pass and that the sufferer will reach a point of being over the grief. Grief is thus allowed a certain period of emotional indulgence before "moving on" is expected.

There is a hint, albeit sentimentally, of a remembering practice in the reference to "bright memories" playing a central role in dispelling sadness. But this idea is not developed far and the overall thrust of the message is that psychological health is best achieved by feeling the loss in a way that leads to catharsis or to decathexis. It is indeed not easy to find a bereavement card that supports remembering practices.

*   *   *

In this chapter we have analyzed a range of pieces of text from different genres that represent the dominant discourse of death and grief in the modern world. Our coverage has not been exhaustive by any means. Nor are our readings the only possible ones. We hope, however, that we have conveyed some sense of the underlying assumptions that we want to depart from. In the next chapter, we need to lay the groundwork for the philosophical approach that we want to build on.

CHAPTER THREE
Constructing Death

> Re-membering practices provide the opportunity for persons to
> resist thin conclusions about their lives and to engage with others in
> the generation of rich descriptions of the stories of their identity.
>   (Michael White, 1997, p. 62)*

We have raised some questions already about the existing knowledges
that inform professional conversations about death and grief. We have
briefly touched on a few of the historical influences that have shaped
these knowledges. The purpose of doing so is not necessarily to criticize
or undermine but to open up new possibilities for practice. It is now
necessary to articulate this practice further. However, we cannot talk
about practice without also talking about the philosophical assumptions that are inevitably woven into the fabric of conversation. In this
chapter, we shall locate the ideas we want to advance in the context of
a philosophical framework. This is not the place though for a detailed
examination of this framework. This task has been done elsewhere
(Burr, 1995; Fairclough, 1992; Gergen, 1994, 1999; Parker, 1992; White
& Epston, 1990). Our aim will be to sketch these ideas briefly in a
way that acknowledges what has influenced us in these ways of thinking
and to demonstrate how these ideas can be applied to talking about
death and grief.

CONSTRUCTIONISM

The constructionist perspective begins with the assumption that
what we say and how we talk matters. The words we use and the traces
of meaning they carry with them impact on the world in tangible ways.
This is a departure from the more dominant idea in social science that

*Reprinted with permission from Dulwich Centre Publications, Adelaide, Australia.

the words we use can be taken to "represent," more or less neutrally, an underlying reality. This has been called the representationalist assumption (Gergen, 1994, 1999; Wittgenstein, 1958). Much "objective" study of psychology has been built on this assumption.

The constructionist perspective suggests a different view that our words and our talk are not neutral. Rather, they are implicated in our construction of the world. They do more than represent reality; they shape it and constitute it. Moreover, the words that we use when we talk (including the talk done in academic books and articles) are not completely under anyone's individual control. We can only speak in the language available to us in the world of discourse in which we are immersed. So our talk will always contain meanings that are not individual to us. They are brought into our conversation as traces carried along with the words (Bakhtin, 1986) or as patterns of taken-for-granted assumptions that lie in the background of what we say, and without which our words cannot have meaning (Drewery & Winslade, 1997; Fairclough, 1992; Parker, 1992).

In this meaning, death is not just a biological event and grief is not just a "natural" phenomenon. It makes a difference how these things get constructed in discourse because it is through discourse that social reality is actually constituted. The words available to us in our language communities are the tools we have to think with. They continually offer us ready-made thoughts and feelings, because words and meanings are products of cultural and political histories. They are replete with taken-for-granted assumptions about which realities, or whose realities, should be accorded prominence and they carry traces of other conversations into every new context in which they are deployed.

From this perspective, death and grief can never be understood as universally uniform experiences (as they have often appeared in psychological and professional literature). Nor can they be thought of as uniquely individual events or processes, because they are shaped by cultural influences that we share in common with others. Death and grief are always being shaped by discourse in particular contexts and we are only able to speak about them in words that are already pregnant with meaning long before we give birth to our utterances. Moreover, such meanings will influence the actual texture of our experience in much more than minor ways. The meanings that words carry into our thinking and feeling affect our judgments of what is valued in families and relationships and what is not, and therefore what should be mourned and how such mourning should be expressed. In this way, the experience of death and of grief is always a cultural matter, since the discourse that carries meaning is produced in cultural contexts.

But we also know that cultural meanings are not the same from one context to another. Neither are they stable through time. Hence, claims to universal psychological meanings (for example about the stages of grief or the tasks of mourning) should be treated as suspect for any particular person or circumstance. Living cultures are also sites of contest and debate about which meanings will be given prominence. The establishment of meanings happens through such debates and is always politically charged. Meanings can be understood as political in this sense. We are not referring to electoral politics here but to the ongoing struggles between diverse social interests to establish legitimate positions from which to act.

Put simply, how we construct death and grief in our talk makes a big difference to how we experience it. Therefore, we had best take the talk into consideration as much as the biological "reality." We had best pay attention, not just to the experiences of grief but also to the work that the words are doing to shape those experiences. If people are going through psychologically painful or problematic times around the presence of death, it may well be that the meanings they are calling on to make sense of life are implicated in the construction of that experience as painful. It may not be death itself so much as the meanings of death that swirl around them that make things painful. If this is the case, it also follows that the introduction of fresh ways of speaking, alternative meaning systems and new narratives can produce altered and enriched experience. That should be the aim of professionals working in this field—to assist people to construct the most helpful and satisfying sets of meanings around the personal and social transitions that death demands.

It is tempting to talk about death as some kind of ultimate reality that transcends culture. This is not an uncommon perspective. And to be sure, death is an undeniable physical event. But even this meaning of death is made in and through discourse, as it always must be, and therefore it is cultural and political. We cannot escape discourse. Reality can only be known through discourse and, therefore, we can say that discourse mediates our experience of physical reality. We can only know about death or about grief within the limits of the "language games" (Wittgenstein, 1958) that we are immersed in.

KNOWLEDGE/POWER

Since the "Enlightenment," the dominant scientific tradition has led us to place a particular emphasis on the project of separating reality from fiction, fact from opinion, objective truth from the fallibility of myth and story. From a constructionist perspective, this project is highly questionable with regard to whether it is either possible or desirable. Many critiques have been mounted of even fundamental psychological knowledge on the basis of the impossibility of transcending social positioning in patterns of, for example, gender and cultural relations.

Despite these critiques, the knowledge that gets produced and legitimated in the academic psychological industry and medical/ scientific exploration has come to inform the practice of professional conversation and eventually lay understandings. In this way, knowledge comes to play a powerful role in the production of people's lives. We can see this happening every day in television talk shows, where constructions of the world that have their origins in academic knowledge are traded back and forth. It is not uncommon to hear all sorts of people reference their brushes with death in ways that would not have been possible even a few decades ago, before the development of modern psychological knowledge about death and grief. People commonly make use of metaphors like the "stages" of grief, the task of "saying good-bye," and the search for "closure." That these words are metaphors produced within particular social contexts, rather than hard facts, seems scarcely to be noticed or questioned.

Constructionist thinking urges us to pay attention to the work that these words are doing, the particular forms of life that are being privileged, the world that is being birthed in the process. We suggest that it is not uniformly helpful. It would be surprising if it were so, given the differences that we know to exist in the world. We should be prepared for people to tell us that existing psychological knowledge is at times constraining for them, that it does not fit well with their position in life, that it seems to apply to some aspects of their grief but not to others.

It is not uncommon nowadays for people to bring a family member, perhaps a child, to a counselor and to announce that they are concerned about this person because he or she is not "grieving properly." They may suggest that there is something wrong because that person has not yet cried about the death of a grandparent, or seems to have been in denial about it. The child may be sitting there bemused by this suggestion and wishing to be somewhere else.

We would suggest that particular forms of psychological knowledge are operating in the background to construct and establish a norm in awkward situations like this. These commonplace conversations did not appear out of a vacuum. There are strong historical roots that shape and design this discourse as we highlighted in Chapter Two. What were originally designed as descriptive studies (for example, Kübler-Ross's

1969 study) became prescriptive accounts of a healthy approach to dying. These prescriptions were further extrapolated to the process of grief after someone dies as well. It has now become almost obligatory, in some cultural contexts, for people to measure their own and their family members' responses to death in comparison with an established norm. Without the existence of the background knowledge, such as that of Kübler-Ross's stages, the assessment of individuals as doing well or not in the grief stakes could not be made.

It is this movement of knowledge from description of experience to prescription of norms, and then regulation of people's lives in relation to such norms, that has been critiqued by Michel Foucault (1980). Foucault was interested in the function of knowledge and discourse in the production of social life and in the construction of power relations. Through the development and deployment of psychological knowledge, we produce identities for people and then squeeze them into performances of identity that fit a given social norm. Thus, the production of "normal" and "natural" grief responses gets built into the production of the normal and stable good citizen of the modern nation state. Such a person will "work through" their grief and "achieve closure" in order to "move on" as expeditiously as possible (without unseemly haste) and resume life as a productive and responsible citizen.

If we experience problems returning to normal, productive citizenship, psychiatric and counseling services are available to remedy the situation. There is a catch, though. In order to access such services, we are often required to adopt an identity construction as in deficit, as slightly less than normal and healthy. We may be described in terms of an "arrested grief reaction," "complicated grief," or "post-traumatic stress syndrome." In other words, the psychological "gaze" (Foucault, 1978) settles usually on finding something wrong with the person and looks to the individual (rather than the relational context) as broken and in need of fixing. The term, "gaze," refers to the sophisticated operation of disciplinary power in the modern world, whereby people are subjected to social control through surveillance. If I think I may be watched and assessed, I am more likely to produce myself to fit a social norm. It is rare for anyone to ask whether the knowledge that informs such professional judgment is faulty, or limited, or culturally inappropriate.

A constructionist perspective requires us to take a different view. For a start, we can always include the discourse that informs experience as part of that experience. We can ask what work is being done by the words in the construction of problematic experiences and be prepared to find that the words are limiting people from living and grieving in ways that they would prefer. In such instances, we can work with people to unpack, or deconstruct, the accepted knowledges and undermine their universalizing "truths." For example, we can spend time talking with the parents who are concerned about a child's "failure" to show expected displays of grief about how they have arrived at such conclusions. Such a move can allow us space to then speak with the child about how they are going about honoring a dead grandparent in his or her own way. In the process, possibilities can be spoken into existence for doing grief, or honoring a dead family member, in ways that could not be envisaged under the regime of standard psychological knowledge.

HOW DO WE WANT TO TELL
THE STORY?

If all the above sounds heavy with the philosophy of language, there is another way we can access these ideas. That is through the use of the narrative metaphor. We are all familiar with the concept of stories. A narrative approach to making sense of life suggests that we pay attention to the work that stories do to shape how people live. The approach to conversations with the dying and the bereaved that we are elaborating here is influenced by work that has been done in narrative theory (Bruner, 1986, 1990; Sarbin, 1986) and in some narrative approaches to therapy (Anderson, 1997; Freedman & Combs, 1996; Monk, Winslade, Crocket, & Epston, 1997; Neimeyer, 2000, 2001; White, 1989, 1997; White & Epston, 1990; Zimmerman & Dickerson, 1996). So let us briefly outline a narrative perspective to death.

The narrative perspective suggests that we live our lives according to story. We perform the practices of living according to how we story ourselves and our lives. To do this, we listen to the stories from the world around us and borrow motifs and characterizations to incorporate in the unfolding story of our own lives. Stories have plot trajectories that carry us along and motivate our actions. They have thematic elements that we draw upon to give meaning to the events of our lives. If we have a storied sense of ourselves as "a failure," for example, then this theme might be produced, or selected over other themes, repeatedly in various contexts. If we are influenced by a story of death as the final act of life during which healthy psychological functioning requires that we say good-bye to our loved ones, we perform acts that support this narrative. From a narrative perspective, *how we tell the story matters*. The story contains within it meanings that make a difference to how we feel and how we act.

However, there is another side to this perspective. If we are shaped by stories as much as by realities, then it is also possible for us to shape our experience differently through telling the story differently. In narrative, we have options for how we tell the meaning of death. We have options about what part of death we want to speak about. We have options about how we want our own death told. And we have options about how we want to construct grief and bereavement in our lives.

From a narrative perspective, then, professional conversations with the dying and bereaved are going to concentrate on the relationship between personal experience and the narratives that are informing that experience. Helping people negotiate the transitions that death proposes will mean helping people access the narratives that are going to be most meaningful and comforting for them, or that will constitute their experience in the ways that they prefer (rather than in ways laid down by dominant knowledge regimes). As we shall see, the boundaries of ownership for narratives are blurred between individuals, and families and communities.

IT'S ALL IN THE RELATIONSHIP

One of the constructionist challenges to the dominant knowledges of psychology is focused on the place of the individual self. Conventional Western thought has placed a great emphasis on the individual self as the origin of thought and action. In most psychological theories, and in most therapies, the individual is assumed to be the prime mover in the construction of his or her own life. On the basis of these assumptions, personality theories have been developed, individual differences have been documented and individual psychotherapy has evolved. Once we start to ask questions about the place of narratives, or discourses, in the construction of experience, the largely exclusive focus of psychology on the individual cannot be sustained. We need to take much more account of how people's personal worlds are constructed in relations with others. We need to place more emphasis on relationships as originary of experience, rather than emphasizing individual intentions as originary of relationships and communities.

There are a number of places we can look for assistance in making this shift. One of them is the tradition of family therapy, which has developed the idea of the family as more than a group of individuals. It has been described rather as a "system" which influences individual responses (Hoffman, 1981; McGoldrick & Gerson, 1985; Minuchin, 1984), or more recently as an "interpretive community"

(Paré, 1996) in which meanings are developed that shape family members' experience.

The Russian literary theorist, Mikhail Bakhtin (1981, 1986), has championed a dialogical perspective, rather than a monological one, for the understanding of human motives and actions. From this perspective, it is always necessary to locate an individual response in the context of some ongoing dialogue(s), rather than to account for it in terms of the individual's own psychology. Life, for Bakhtin, is an ongoing stream of never-ending dialogues. Moreover, each utterance in any dialogue contains traces of other conversations in other times and places. Says Bakhtin (1981):

> . . . the word . . . exists in other people's mouths, in other people's contexts, serving other people's intentions. . . . Language is not a medium that passes freely and easily into the private property of the speaker's intentions; it is populated—overpopulated—with the intentions of others (pp. 293-294).

One corollary of this idea is that biological death does not equate with silence. People's voices continue to be heard after death in the traces of their utterances, in other people's speaking, and in ongoing responses to their words. For the living, this means that, to the degree that we continue to respond to the meanings generated in conversation with someone before they died, those meanings continue to live. In a quite tangible sense, people can live on after death in and through words and our relationships with the dead need not be considered closed with the nailing down of the lid of a coffin.

Sheila McNamee and Ken Gergen (1999) have argued for a relational perspective on responsibility, a domain conventionally considered in individual terms. From a relational perspective, meaningful language is always constructed in the process of a relationship. Therefore, relationship deserves the prime position in our accounts of thought, ahead of the individual mind. On this view, our thoughts, feelings, words, and actions (including our experiences of dying and grieving) are all co-constructed with those around us, rather than originating within the individual. Roughly speaking, this is a more outside-in than inside-out, psychology. As we interact with each other, we create discourse that shapes our internal experience. Meanings are therefore primary products of relational exchanges, rather than direct products of reality itself or emergent from the deep psyche of the individual.

When we think in this way, the story of death and bereavement changes from many conventional understandings. The host of particular meanings that accompany an experience of death need to be understood as produced within the network of relationships in which the death is experienced. The degree of emphasis on such meanings as "blessed relief" or "tragic loss" are loosened from their essential attachment to death itself and referenced to the relational exchanges in which they are being generated. The advantage of this perspective is that it renders the meaning of death much more fluid and available to shifts in relational exchanges. The conversations that professionals have with their clients can therefore be opened up to a much more creative function. The professional task becomes not simply helping people work through grief processes prescribed by nature, but helping them shape the meanings that will govern their experience. Helping people reach acceptance gives way to helping them construct meanings which will sustain them through the transitions that death demands.

IMPLICATIONS FOR REMEMBERING

The question that arises at this point is about the implications of the social constructionist framework that we have outlined for the remembering conversations that we are advocating. We shall close this chapter by considering this question.

If we are prepared to set aside the realist and representationalist assumptions of conventional modernist discourse, then remembering conversations take on an added potential. They become places where relationships are being constructed, knowledges are being performed, and cultures elaborated. Remembering is not simply a nostalgic pastime. Nor is it about living in the past and losing relevance for today. It is about affirming membership, cultural belonging, and discursive agency. Remembering is an active process at the edge of where discourse gets to be formed.

Grieving, too, becomes an active process, although not in Worden's sense of completing some required tasks. It is active in the sense that it is about the deliberate construction of relationship and community, through which participants will form identity in the future. It is a cultural project, rather than a natural phenomenon.

Constructionism does not require us to jettison completely all extant psychological theories of dying and grieving. But it does require us to view them as products of discourse in particular contexts. This means that at times they do have useful value in their context. But it also alerts us to the dangers of assuming that such value is universal or uniform. It takes stages of grief and grief tasks down off their normative pedestal and places them much lower in the hierarchy of knowledge.

The ideas of membership and remembering conversation should not be placed on high pedestals either. They, too, are simply pieces of knowledge created at a particular historical juncture in response to modernist trends in the practice of death. Different emphases will no doubt emerge in the future.

An implication for professional practice of this approach to psychological knowledge is that we should take care not to squeeze people's lives into our current theories in the name of psychology. This has happened far too often in recent decades. It is often not respectful. Rather, professionals working with the dying and bereaved should learn to be far more curious about what those they are serving find comforting, sustaining, and enlivening. They should invite people more often into the role of making meaning of their own experience, rather than interpreting their experience for them to fit with theory.

In this kind of work, stories take on a much greater importance than scientific truths. They become the stuff of identity projects, of relational belonging, and of cultural resonance. In an important sense, stories are the medium through which we live, love, and grieve. We believe that remembering conversations give the stories that shape our lives a more prominent place from which to do their work.

Finally, let us note that stories are products of culture. And respect for cultural belonging has been severely constrained under the modernist regime. We have been constantly invited to view ourselves, and each other, primarily as individuals, rather than as members of cultural contexts. Inevitably, theories of grief have focused on individual processes, rather than on cultural stories. Despite a Western trend to teach "cultural sensitivity," the language and rituals around death for families from cultural minorities have often been left with the short end of the comparative stick.

It is time for professionals to offer more respect for the ways in which different cultural traditions offer people pathways through the transitions that death calls us into. We believe that remembering conversations place culturally significant rituals and stories in positions of greater prominence and support their incorporation in the life of the dying and the bereaved.

In this chapter we have opened the theoretical door. We need to step through it now, in order to articulate a practice. In subsequent chapters, we shall address some innovative ways to include and respect the polysemy of differing cultural stories and practices. The practice of remembering conversation will be described before death, in the presence of death, and on down through the years after a loved one has died.

CHAPTER FOUR
Death Doesn't Mean Saying Good-bye

> How much of him there remains in what he touched and what he named; in the hours of the day, in the flowers and animals, in the verdure of the woods, in the autumn sky.
>
> *Boris Pasternak to T.G. Yashvili on the death of her husband, 28 August 1937* (Harding & Dyson, 1981, p.155)*

Good-byes are tricky for most of us. When we love somebody, the thought of being apart for an extended period is not comfortable. We miss their physical presence and the sound of their voice. We wonder how they are and look forward to hearing from them again. It is normal for most people to not want to be apart from those that they love for any length of time, although life requires us to do this at many times. The experience of "missing" is not usually invigorating, in spite of aphorisms about absence making the heart grow fonder.

Part of our discomfort comes from not quite knowing how to manage periods of missing. We do not have a readily available discourse that offers helpful suggestions about how to navigate this experience. We can pine and mourn and wallow, all of which leaves us in less comfortable places than where we started. What seems to be absent from the discourse of missing are helpful constructions that allow us to utilize the absence in a way that affirms relationship. Although the greeting card industry has provided "I wish you were here" cards, the absence usually is construed as a lack of something, or somebody, rather than as a new context in which relationship might develop.

---

*From *A Book of Condolences: Classic Letters of Bereavement,* edited by Rachel Harding and Mary Dyson, © 1981 by the editors. Reprinted by permission of The Continuum Publishing Group.

Now imagine that the leave-taking is more dramatic. When a person is dying, we are asked to say good-bye. We are put into a position that often was uncomfortable throughout life and are asked to exaggerate this experience into one final act of separation. We act as if this is the ultimate farewell; the one that all the other "so longs" were in preparation for. For the dying person, the farewells can be very daunting if we ask them to say "good-bye" to *all* their acquaintances, friends, family, pets, and favorite places, foods, belongings, and memories. Ritual severance from things that we hold dear can potentially produce unnecessary hardship and emotional suffering. Saying good-bye can suggest to the person who is dying that after their deaths we will write them out of our script—the script that previously featured them variously in starring or supporting roles. We infer that because good-byes have been said, the dying person is no longer needed, and can proceed to take their journey away from those that are loved.

For the family and friends of the person who is dying, the thought of such finality can be equally hard to bear. To think that life will mean going on without their loved one can be heart-breaking. For years we may have built our lives and identities to be intertwined with a spouse or a child or a dear friend. We may have known them for 30 or 60 years. They have played a significant role in our stories of who we are. To say a final good-bye can amount to acting as though their contribution to our stories no longer matters. In some circumstances, this distancing can be harmful to those who remain alive. On the other hand, bringing to life those who have died and keeping a person's memory alive can be life-saving. The following story illustrates this point.

Jannette and Nicholas loved each other very much. Nicholas did not want Jannette to die and stated this loudly. When I (Lorraine) would meet with them, she would say, "Nicholas we have to talk about this."

And he always said the same thing, "I don't want to talk about it!"

Both were from New York and they spoke in an animated and boisterous way which was exaggerated by the fact that neither of them could hear very well. In between gripes about her desire to talk and his desire not to, they would burst into their favorite Frank Sinatra tune and serenade each other with loud, off-key melodies. These conversations were very lively, even in the midst of difficult arguments.

Jannette was genuinely concerned about Nicholas. On a number of occasions, Nicholas had mentioned that, upon her death, he was planning to kill himself. He could not imagine life without his lovely wife and had decided to shoot himself. The morning Jannette died, Nicholas became agitated and was yelling at the hospice staff. I was paged to the inpatient unit, where Nicholas and I talked, next to the bed where Jannette's dead body lay.

He told me how he could not go on and how Jannette had brought life to him. "It feels like my life is over," he said.

I asked him questions to strengthen Jannette's voice and presence within him. I wanted him to have an understanding that he could still have connection with her. Otherwise, I feared that he might kill himself. For a couple of hours, we talked about the times they had shared together, the laughter and the disagreements. He told me about how they had always said they were only a half of person without the other one, and that half of her lived in him and half of him lived in her. I took this metaphor as an invitation and asked him many more questions about it.

"How would the half of her that lives in you want you to carry on?"

"What might the half of her that lives in you say about how you can do well at this?"

"What might the half of her that lives in you want Nicholas to remember about the times you both have shared?"

Nicholas answered by singing another Sinatra tune. He explained that "What are you doing the rest of your life?" was one of Jannette's favorite songs.

I asked, "How would she like you to answer that now Nicholas?"

He replied, "She'd want me to keep singing."

This story is about the refusal to accept the customary notion that death requires relationships to end. For Nicholas, it was imperative that we bring Jannette to life. Had we insisted that he say good-bye, I question whether he would still be living two years after her death. Jannette had been a primary club member in Nicholas' life. It was critical, not only to acknowledge her importance, but also to renew her membership card in his life at the time she died. By bringing forth her voice, stories, songs and presence we were inviting her membership status to remain viable for the immediate future, as well as for the long term.

When somebody dies, those who will continue on have the opportunity to review their membership with the deceased. It is a less common circumstance where a person needs to be written out or distanced from membered status following death. We will address some of these occasions later in chapter ten. For the purposes of this chapter, we will focus on membership in contexts where people want to maintain the connection with the person who has died. It was important for Nicholas to know he still had Jannette's membership card with him. He needed to not have it expire at the time she died, but to renew and renegotiate their love.

LOVE MEANS NEVER HAVING
TO SAY GOOD-BYE

When we love someone, we enjoy being in their presence. However, we are also able to carry them with us throughout our day. When we are away at work or a loved one has gone to the grocery store, we do not stop loving that person, simply because we cannot see her or him for a period of time. We are able to hold this connection intact in our hearts. In their absence for short or longer periods, we do not call into question their membership in our club of life. In fact, if required, we could conjure up their image and words with little effort since we know them well enough. Death does not need to change this. The people we know and love can be said to be always right with us, whether present in body or not. Joseph Campbell (1988) wrote about his realization of this idea:

> I've lost a lot of friends, as well as my parents. A realization has come to me very, very keenly, however, that I haven't lost them. That moment when I was with them has an everlasting quality about it that is now still with me. What it gave me then is still with me, and there's a kind of intimation of immortality in that (p. 228).

We do not have to be caught in the realist assumption that if the other person is not present and visible to us then the relationship no longer exists. We teach young children to learn that a parent going out of the room is not going out of their lives. The childhood game of peekaboo is a basic teaching tool for this lesson. As children grow, they learn to handle transitions that occur as parents leave the house and return. We learn that out of sight does not have to equate with out of mind. As we age into adolescence and adulthood, we know that membership continues, even with people with whom we are not physically in contact. We amass literally hundreds of examples of friends, teachers, and relatives with whom we are able to stay in relationship without being in their physical presence every waking minute.

Modernist psychology has defined this human trait as the ability to form attachments. It gives us the capability of remaining attached when we are not physically connected. We would suggest a more relational revision of the concept of "attachment" that constructs it more as a product of relationship and less as an individual developmental task. When we see life from the perspective of membership, we are free not to believe that death must mean the negation of attachment. Rather, we can continue living in an "attached" position, just as we do when our loved one is away on a trip. At the same time, we can continue to acknowledge that membership is fluid and alive and that it sometimes ebbs or may even be revoked. Death does not supercede membership status by requiring us to disavow our affiliations with our deceased loved one. Death only asks us to reincorporate membership in new ways.

Artificial good-byes are not necessary. They do not reflect how connections continue to matter and live on. There are times, as with Jannette and Nicholas, that it might actually be detrimental to force a severance of this connection. For most of us, disavowing our connections does not feel loving or affirming. If we can extract death out from under the sway of the metaphor of good-bye, then we can open more life-affirming possibilities.

Michael White (1989) couched a description of these possibilities in the metaphor of "saying hullo again." Rather than building utterances and rituals around cutting someone off, we can look for places of inclusion and continuity. Rather than requiring the breaking of bonds, we can seek out opportunities for them to continue (Klass et al., 1996). Death does require that we acknowledge a relational transition. As Thomas Attig (2001) comments, in the wake of death, ". . . reciprocity changes. We continue to give and to receive. They continue to give us their legacies" (p. 46). The old relationship does not continue in the same corporeal way. It has to be reincorporated or re-embodied. The transition that death requires can, therefore, be thought of as a process of re-incorporation of the old relationship in some new forms, precisely so that it can continue. To achieve this transition, we need to be creative about designing ways to reincorporate the dead in our thoughts, in our conversations, and in our rituals of living.

A colleague of John's offered this story by way of illustration. Ten years after the death of her father she still treasures one card that she was sent because of its contrast with the other messages received at the time. She writes:

> Today I only remember one card specifically. Its message was transforming at the time, because it encouraged me to, not only acknowledge the loss of my father, which I was constantly doing, but also to remember the joy and happiness I had brought to him. This I had not thought of.

The message on the card that struck this chord says:

> May it bring some consolation
> To remember, too,
> How many times your loved one found
> Great happiness in you.

The message was one that did not direct her focus toward the experience of loss but toward the experience of a relationship and the remembering of its joyful aspects (unlike the sympathy card referred to in Chapter Two). That the message is still continuing to serve this purpose 10 years on is attested to by this story. The messages that focused her attention on loss have no doubt dropped away and been forgotten.

TALKING TO THE DEAD

Many studies point to practices that maintain connection following death. Shuchter (1986) suggests that spouses frequently maintain connection by dreaming about, talking with, or simply sensing the deceased's presence in the years following death. Shapiro (1994) states that the continued reincorporation of the deceased's image and presence serves to benefit the strength of the living family. Mary Gergen (1987) refers to the importance of "social ghosts" which are "real or fictitious persons with whom individuals conduct imaginal interactions over time; they are the cast of characters with whom we engage in imaginal dialogues" (Stroebe et al., 1996, p. 41). Many people speak with their deceased loved ones on a daily basis. They may write letters to them, dream of them, or feel their presence in their activities and projects. They might be living in the home that they shared with the person who has died and have physical reminders all around them. One woman shared with me (Lorraine) how seeing her husband's name on her checks the month following his death comforted her.

"He would have wanted me to not have to worry about finances after he died. He worked hard all his life in hopes that we would be all right in our retirement. Having his name on the checks reminds me that he is still looking after me in that way," she said.

Nowhere is this sensing of the deceased more poignant than with children whose parent has died. Silverman and Nickman (1996) questioned 125 children, aged 6 to 17, after the death of a parent. Most of the children's responses were about how the children were constructing connections with their dead parent. The five primary ways in which the children accomplished this connection were: "locating" the deceased (having a sense of their whereabouts—often in heaven); experiencing the deceased (feeling them close by); reaching out to the deceased to initiate a connection (speaking to them or visiting the cemetery); remembering (reminiscing and waking memories); and, keeping an object or something that belonged to the deceased as a way of linking with them (Silverman & Nickman, 1996, pp. 73-86). Such research supports the value for children of ongoing relationships with the deceased. Despite the prevalence of these practices, however, many people know instinctively the strong cultural pressure to move on. Well-intentioned friends might take up the cultural banner by unintentionally silencing stories and remembrances. They might offer distractions from thinking about deceased loved ones, or change the topic whenever their names are mentioned. A young woman explained to us how only four months after her husband's death, her family never mentions his name. Accounts such as these are commonplace, even though they are in sharp contrast with the experience of the many bereaved people who report feeling as though their loved one is all around them.

We hear numerous stories from newly bereaved people about how they can hear the deceased's voice, have dreams that feel as though they are "in the room," smell their perfume, or simply notice a calming sense as if "she is sitting on my shoulder." Often these stories are prefaced by, "You might think this is crazy, but. . . ." People know that common discursive understandings might banish these experiences to the psychotic or paranormal, rather than including them as ordinary aspects of death. Inviting people to speak about these experiences can produce validation for the sanity of maintaining connections in the face of death, rather than craziness.

There are many cultural contexts where this idea does not sound so unusual as it does when colonized by a "rational," scientifically validated approach to life. I (John) have experienced this in relation to Maori cultural perspectives in New Zealand. For Maori, it is quite ordinary for people to think, "The dead are always with us." In Maori greeting rituals, the dead are always mentioned alongside the living. And it is not uncommon for people to talk with those who have died. A story illustrates the degree to which this practice is natural within Maori culture.

A colleague with a commitment to narrative therapy was talking with a counselor who was Maori. The conversation had come around to the subject of the Maori counselor's mother, who had died some years earlier. He spoke about how he continues to consult with her when he faces a troubling decision in life. He puts the issue to her and then waits to hear her reply. Her voice in his head sooner or later arrives with a comment from her perspective. My colleague saw the connection with the process that has developed a literature around it called "internalized other" conversations (see below). This is the process whereby counselors ask clients to have a conversation with the internalized voices of significant others.

"Do you know we have a word for that in narrative therapy?" says my colleague. "We call it *internalized other conversations.*"

"Really," says the Maori counselor, slightly underwhelmed. "I just call it talking to my mother."

For him, this was such a familiar aspect of ongoing relationship with a dead loved one that it did not need a fancy psychological name to legitimize it.

TALKING ABOUT THE DEAD

Encouraging people to speak about past events is like harvesting the fruits of a lifetime. These fruits can provide sustenance during the transition into a future in which the deceased is accorded an important place of membership.

One woman mentioned how, two months after her husband had died, her friends were very attentive and took her to the movies or to dinner. When there was talk of her husband, the friends would become upset and reassure her that she did not need to talk about him. She found this odd and disquieting. In response, she brought up his name and opinion whenever possible. She found herself saying when they were out, "Oh, Hank would have loved that movie," or, "I recall when Hank and I were at this restaurant last year."

Rather than colluding with her friends' unintentional efforts to cut off her husband's membership, she actively sought to remember him by including his stories and presence. She hoped that as she continued to bring him into conversation, her friends would also grow increasingly more comfortable speaking about him.

Ongoing inclusion of the deceased in conversation offers comfort to those managing the transition that comes with death. Rather than waking up to a stark reality of loss, they can find their loved one's ongoing presence in the daily events of life. Others can assist this by joining in the reintroduction of the dead person into conversation and by continuing to share stories that invoke the dead person's memory. The renegotiation of relationship happens through a thousand such moments. If we are fortunate, we might have discussed some of the stories to be highlighted with our loved one prior to their death and consulted with them about their preferences. However, many people die without notice or are unable to have these conversations. Families then can utilize the wealth of knowledge they have collected about the person. Family members usually have a strong sense about what mattered to their loved ones, and can breathe life into memories on behalf of the dead.

The process of reincorporating the membership of the dead person can begin immediately. No time lag is required, as with some conventional models of grief and bereavement. We do not have to wait for some arbitrary time to pass until we can make major decisions or feel "healed." We do not need to feel the loss to some satisfactory degree of intensity, or even acknowledge the reality of death. Membership is an ongoing state that is not stopped or started when a person dies. Membership can be visualized on a map that connects our membership with a network of relationships woven around our deceased loved one. On the map's legend are keys to the good times we have shared, markers of change and growth, physical reminders and dearly recalled events that were important to our friend. These reference points can direct us to understand the relationship further and to create a sense of belonging with this person in the future.

One family I (Lorraine) met with after the death of their father shared such a story. The brother and sister told how they had shared caregiving responsibilities for their father for a few months through the course of a degenerative illness. After his death, they had tended to his belongings and had decided that his many pets would be divided to live in their homes. Their father had always enjoyed animals and had had many pets throughout his life and had passed on this love of animals to his children. It was something that they all shared and valued. During the week immediately after his death, a white dove kept hanging around his porch. While the children were busy sorting his belongings, the dove would wait outside on their father's chair. As if to call them out to the porch, it sat patiently day after day. Whenever the brother and sister would sit out there, as they had done with their father, the bird would sit with them. Soon, they almost jokingly took to calling the bird by their father's name.

When I spoke with them, they wondered whether it could be a messenger from their father or whether perhaps he had been reincarnated as this dove. They fed it and cared for it, as they had done so carefully for their dad. A couple of weeks later, when they were done with sorting their father's house, the bird flew off.

Stories about connecting, in whatever form they might come, seem to provide great comfort. We are always in the process of making meanings. Death often calls us to reassess the meanings and purpose of our lives. What once made sense and appeared secure can be shaken by the event of death. Many have written about the importance of meaning in everyday living and extrapolated this to the changes that often occur when death enters life (Frankl, 1959, 1978; Neimeyer, 2001). Attig (1996) suggests,

. . . the learning and relearning involve investment of ourselves as whole persons, in all facets of our life all at once, as we learn how to be ourselves in the world before. . . . We strive to adapt our behaviors and daily life patterns to new life circumstances not of our choosing and to recover our sense of daily purpose (pp. 13-14).

INTERNAL REPRESENTATIONS
OF THE DEAD

We come to know our loved ones well during the time that we are with them. We gauge their responses and can anticipate their answers often before they speak. As we are growing up we effortlessly learn this ability with our parents and siblings. As children, we progress from having our parents tell us to not step in front of moving cars, to carrying their voices with us as we make daily decisions to cross streets. This internalization becomes a vital tool to guide us and assist us in far more complex situations than negotiating traffic. Although these dialogues seem like we are "talking to ourselves," we can also think of them as relational performances.

The dialogue that occurs in conversation is readily transplanted to an inner dialogue. We have the amazing ability to conjure and create the voice, wisdom, and knowledge of another in our own head. Most of what we call our own thoughts are echoes of these internal voices and dialogues that are with us at all times. When we think narratively, we are free to access and utilize the gifts of these internal dialogues. They are especially valuable when death threatens to reduce our utterances to a monologue.

People tell us frequently, "It is as if my loved one were right here." We can continue to have them living and conversing with us, almost as if in daily dialogue.

For others whose loved one has died, the cultural forces we have mentioned often take a toll on their ability to recognize and grow these dialogues. They may feel very distant from their connection and struggle to hear the voice of their loved one. For these people, as well as for those who can readily access their loved one's voices, we would suggest that it is important to bring forward their inner knowledge. We want people to be able to locate their loved ones within them, just as much as we want them to locate their loved ones in family and community. One particularly helpful way we can do this is by "speaking" with, or interviewing, those who live on through internal representation.

INTERVIEWING INTERNALIZED OTHERS

The practice of interviewing the internalized other has developed in family therapy especially in relation to couples in conflict (Epston, 1993; Tomm, 1996; Winslade & Monk, 2000). It involves interviewing one member of a relationship and asking them to speak in the voice of the other. What the speaker is then giving voice to is her or his internalized version of the other person's voice.

We find that there is a particular value in the context of remembering conversation for such interviewing. Surviving family members can be invited to give voice to what a dead person might say and, in this way, keep their voice alive. In some situations, a whole conversation with a dead person might be held through asking questions of their loved ones that invite them to speak in the voice of the dead person.

Here is an example of an internalized voice from someone who had died ten years previously.

> Justine: Today a funny thing happened. I was just doing some things, taking the rubbish out, before I came out. And I heard in the back of my head, "Take your slippers off before you go outside, girl, or you'll get them all dirty." And it was my mother's voice.
>
> John: Still giving you advice?
>
> Justine: Yeah, or "Don't come in the house with those dirty shoes on." It's the practicalities. Every time I make a certain recipe, I think of my mother. She taught me heaps of practical things.

Notice the sense of present tense in this exchange. I was concerned in my use of the word "still" to reference the voice of Justine's mother in the present tense, rather than to assign it to the past. I did this in order to acknowledge that an internalized utterance like this continues to live and do its work in shaping material decisions, long after the person who originally uttered it is dead. I was not wishing to refer to it as a voice from the past, or as a throwback, or give it a pathological meaning as an introjected parental injunction from which Justine needed to free herself. Rather, I heard this voice as an ongoing resource for living and wanted to recognize it and validate it as such. In this way, Justine's mother was remembered.

In this instance, the internalized voice just popped up. In other instances, it can be useful to ask for its appearance. Here are some examples of questions that might be asked to invite out a conversation with an internalized other.

- Mary, what do you think Keith would say if I could ask him, "How is Mary doing since you died?"
- If Keith was to give you advice about this decision that you are struggling with, what would he say?
- What sorts of things would Keith say it would mean to him to watch his daughter graduate?
- What kinds of expressions would he use in situations like this?

Each of these questions invites a response that is double-voiced (Bakhtin, 1986). It includes the person who has died as an ongoing presence with opinions and advice to offer and positions the speaker as someone who has a meaningful ongoing relationship with them. Therefore, the practice of internalized other questioning fits well within the context of remembering conversations.

RITUALS THAT HELP US REMEMBER

Rituals can show us the way in times of change. By "ritual" we mean practices that involve the performance of meaning (Bruner, 1986; Myerhoff, 1978, 1982, 1986). Anthropologists have described the ways in which culturally sanctioned rituals serve the purpose of marking the rites of passage that we move through as we transition from one social status, or one identity, to another (van Gennep, 1960). They may be practices that are apparently ordinary, like the cleaning of a house, or complex and elaborate performances such as the public displays of political and military ritual that accompanied the funeral of Britain's Queen Mother in 2002. Rituals can mark what is changed in a relationship following death, and they can invite us to reincorporate the past relationship in new forms of living. In the process, they can cement our connections with those who have passed away.

Often, we look to a memorialization or funeral to do just this. These are public rituals in which we can bring forward stories and acknowledge relationships in our club of life. We encourage people to create funerals that grow connections and that facilitate the re-incorporation of the dead in our ongoing lives. There is a lot of satisfaction in creating a gathering where people come away knowing more about their loved one than before the gathering. Often people grow new understandings of the dead through hearing stories from multiple perspectives. Family and friends gather and speak about the person who 20 or 50 years ago was very different from in the last 10 years. Families and friends frequently come away from a funeral saying they never knew this or that tidbit about the person who died.

Rituals can also take many quite particular forms too. They can be created in relation to the circumstances of the relationship with the deceased and the death. In New Zealand in recent years, it has become the practice to mark the site at which people die on the highway in road accidents with a white cross. Family members will often decorate these crosses with flowers. These practices have been popular in Arizona as well. Historically, markers were placed to signify a place were a person's soul left his or her body. Now they have come to stand for much more than personal reminders of death. These are simple acts of remembering that serve also as reminders to other drivers on the road of the dangers of road accidents. It is an example of a ritual that has ongoing social and political significance.

Another ritual that has political significance developed in the United States during the AIDS epidemic among gay men. This was the ritual of conducting vigils alongside the person who lay dying (Richards, 2001). Music and candles and pictures of the dying person were used to invoke an atmosphere of spiritual meaning. This practice enabled a community of friends to gather in solidarity around a dying man, sometimes in circumstances where homophobic rigidity was isolating this person from being fully membered in family networks. As a social practice, this ritual served several purposes. It affirmed membership, stood up to other practices of dismemberment, and enabled relationships to be reincorporated into new forms, as death required.

REMEMBERING CONVERSATIONS

Remembering conversations can be opportunities to "say hullo again" (White, 1989). It is important that professionals assist people's noticing of these moments and help grow them larger. We need to ask questions about the meanings, the surprises, the cherished moments and the new-found ideas that establish and affirm relationship. Conventional social forces otherwise will take their toll and dissolve connections further, or force unnecessary good-byes.

Therapeutic remembering conversations allow us to separate out various moments and investigate the meanings of events to the person. We might ask, "Is that similar to how you knew your friend, as she was being described at the funeral?" We would intentionally inquire about the personal meanings of others' perceptions. For example, "How is it that so many other people knew him as a person who gave to his family? What might you recall about him that also suggests this possibility?"

At one man's funeral, a time was set aside for sharing stories. I (Lorraine) recall the most wonderful example of a story that worked to connect the deceased with future family practices. A young man who was a friend of the family stood to speak about what he learned from this man over the years.

> When I first met Gilbert, I was only a teenager. I used to visit his son and hang out with them on weekends. I'd watch as his son, who was also a teenager at the time, would kiss his father before we'd go off to our [sports] game. I thought to myself, "Man, this is a little weird," but I never said anything. Gilbert used to say, "Family is the most important thing." I knew this was true for him and he didn't care who saw him kiss his boys or what they would say about it.
>
> As the years went on and they continued to do this, I grew more comfortable with this practice and found myself hugging Gilbert when I would see him. He became like a father to me and it just seemed like the natural thing to do. I was never that close with my own Dad and Gilbert was always right there for me through the thick and thin. Well, wouldn't you know it! Pretty soon, I was also kissing the old man. Never thought anything of it. We told each other that we loved one another, just like I was his son. Now as I look out in the audience, I see my own son. He's twelve now. And I hope to God that I never stop kissing him and telling him that I love him.

Later that week, Gilbert's family spoke about what it meant to hear this story. They knew that Gilbert had this practice with his two sons and bragged about the importance of staying close with family. This was something that they all valued. They explained that this young man's story was testimony to how Gilbert cared for people. It was less of a surprise, they said, than an affirmation of what they loved about him. We spoke, too, about how Gilbert would want them to continue these rituals. I asked what their plans were to affirm the importance of family, as he had done for so many years. They had many ideas about how they could do this besides continuing to demonstrate their love for one another.

CULTURAL DIFFERENCES OF FUNERAL RITES

It is unfortunate that in modernist Western culture funerals are often solemn affairs that do not include much participation from family and friends. It is not uncommon to have a funeral where the minister is the only person who speaks. The minister might highlight a person's spiritual relationship and some salient life events but not be in a position to appreciate the complex multi-hued experiences that reflect the fullness of a person's life.

By contrast, a memorial service can be an occasion that builds a bridge between the living and the dead. It can be a time that shines a light on the future of saying hello rather than saying good-bye. Funerals in other cultures have often created rituals and practices that are affirming of relationships. It is possible to borrow from them in creating new cultural rituals and remembering practices.

Among the Maori of New Zealand, the whanau (or family) will make every effort to surround a person who is dying, so that he or she does not die alone. This practice continues after the death too. A body will not be left alone until it is buried. Says Maori writer, Harry Dansey (1977), ". . . the dead are to be cared for, cherished, mourned, spoken to, honored in a way that others might consider to be over-emotional and over-demonstrative. . . . We stay with them every minute and talk to them and sing to them. When we have returned them to the earth, we remember them in song and speech" (pp. 177, 188). Later, the headstone for the deceased is placed on the gravesite on the first year anniversary of the death, or sometimes up to five years later (Ngata, 1987). Unfortunately, modernist Western culture often does not have similar practices that exist past the time of memorialization. Anniversaries, birthdays, death dates, holidays, and daily events often go by unnoticed. This unnoticing risks producing a dismembering outcome.

Remembering, then, is about the deliberate avoidance of saying good-bye rituals. It is a practice that seeks out opportunity for continuing relationship and that approaches the emergency of death as a time of transition, in which new forms of connection can be forged and existing forms affirmed. We have been speaking of this remembering as a task for the living to attend to. But it has implications for the dying too that we shall turn to in the next chapter.

CHAPTER FIVE
Who Will Carry My Stories?

It was though he possessed some quality stronger than absence
and distance—an essential lovableness and reliability and warmth
that continued to affect one, in spite of the obstacles interposed
by space and time.

Aldous Huxley to Mrs. Martha Saxton on the death of her
husband, 6 July 1943 (Harding & Dyson, 1999, p. 156)*

Nobody wants to be forgotten. This is one important assumption we
keep in mind when speaking with those who are approaching death.
We have briefly introduced how narrative ideas impact on connections
with the dead for those whose loved one has died and will elaborate
further on this in subsequent chapters. There is a certain common sense
in supporting the practice of remembering for those who live on. But
what about for those who are facing death? How can we speak with
them about ongoing membership? How can remembering conversations
be helpful for a person who is about to die?

The key to answering these questions is the idea that the kind of
remembering we promote does not just take place as an event inside
someone's head or as a passing reminiscence. The constructionist
perspective is that significant memories take shape primarily in a
relational space. They are shaped and given meaning in conversation,
in actions and in rituals that we share with others. It is in this often
little-noticed liminal space that we breathe life into all that we do.
Conversation provides a polymer to bind us to what we hold dear.
It fastens together our actions, thoughts, and relationships and gives
us meaning. This chapter is about these shared experiences when

*From *A Book of Condolences: Classic Letters of Bereavement,* edited by Rachel Harding
and Mary Dyson, © 1981 by the editors. Reprinted by permission of The Continuum
Publishing Group.

death is imminent. It is about how to make conversations with the dying sparkle and shine magnificently.

The idea that life can go on in story even after our physical body has died underpins this work. When death is waiting outside the door, special opportunities arise for appreciating this idea. We can let people know that they matter now, and that they will matter for years to come. The threads of a person's influence on those around them can be gathered together and woven into a thick rope of connection. We can select for emphasis the most significant strands of a life and make commitments about how these strands will continue to be woven into the tapestry of life among those who continue to live. The dying can be invited to participate in this process of weaving and can ask for things that they would like to have remembered.

ETHICAL WILLS AND LIFE REVIEWS

First, let us briefly note some practices which support the remembering of people who are dying. There is a small and growing understanding in lay literature of the value of employing an "ethical will." An ethical will can be a single document, or can be composed of many autobiographical elements that pass on personal legacies following death. According to Barry Baines (2002), "Legal wills bequeath *valuables,* while ethical wills bequeath values" (p. 14). He encourages people to construct such documents before their death and pass them as if passing a baton in an intergenerational relay race. The creation of a pre-mortem written legacy can be an affirmative act that enables connection after death. (Ethical wills are not to be confused with "living wills" which are about instructions with regard to resuscitation in the event of sudden serious injury.) While we support such a practice as an entry point, the process of remembering needs to be taken further into the domain of conversation, relationship, and community.

This too can be said regarding the practice of "life review." Life review methods are commonly practiced in England, and have been taken up by many hospice programs. Life review techniques have gained some acceptance and have been incorporated into other practice models. According to Garland (1994), life review is defined as "a process of systematic reflection in later life, with a therapist and client trying to understand a life-history's implications for current coping strategies" (p. 21). As with an ethical will, the emphasis of recollection is on the individual telling their own story. Life reviews are not necessarily aimed at creating legacy or connection to a community, but are geared toward individual meaning-making and reflection. Bornat (1994) distinguishes four aspects of reminiscence: "finding positive memories, confronting painful memories, empowering memories inhibited by grief and encouraging non-narcissistic memories" (pp. 17–18). These methods have been used in nursing homes and hospices to voice the stories of many marginalized individuals. The focus of life reviews still does not anchor membership for the dying in their relationships.

At stake is the affirmation of continued membership for the person who is dying. How will we renew this person's membership card in our "club of life" again and again when death itself threatens to cancel it? Ethical wills and life review practices only begin to scratch the surface of ongoing membership. What we are suggesting is a far more agentic step for the person who is about to die. We want him or her to know who will be in charge of the renewal process and in what form; where and how continuity of honored membership will emerge into fluid remembering practices.

Unlike our library cards, our membership cards need not expire just because we are dead. However, people are often quick to assume that this will be the case. Such an assumption can be challenged, not necessarily through head-on rebuke, but through crafting a conversation built on the assumption that remembering is what everyone wants and that forgetting need not prevail.

CONSTRAINTS ON REMEMBERING

This task of remembering is made easier by most people's willingness to join with it. It appears to us that often the desire to be remembered is a secret wish harbored by those who are dying. They want to talk with loved ones about how this will happen but they also often feel culturally constrained from speaking it out loud. And so do the rest of us. Because of these constraints, we can easily overlook opportunities to speak with the person who is dying about these matters. So what are some of the constraints on remembering conversations?

We may shy away from these conversations for fear of upsetting the dying person. We may not wish to appear too blunt or we may superstitiously imagine that speaking about death can actually cause it to happen. We may also be so focused on the aspect of loss that we neglect a focus on what need not be lost. In this focus, we may be influenced by a psychology that categorizes and evaluates "anticipatory losses" and advises us to privilege and feel intensely our feelings of loss as part of healthy functioning. The suggestion that we should express and not hold in emotions associated with loss appears sometimes to overlook the expression of other feelings than those associated with loss.

When these constraints are operating, it can be hard for the person who is dying to open up important conversations about how they wish to be remembered. Merely speaking about these things can be experienced as opening up unfamiliar cultural nodes of interaction. However, if we remember that people facing death often want the opportunity to speak about dying, then we can be on the alert for openings. Imagine what it might be like to be embarking on a great journey, such as sailing around the world, but not being allowed to tell anyone of your upcoming trip or to find someone to water your plants and feed the cat in your absence.

RON'S STORY: WHAT DOES REMEMBERING MEAN TO SOMEBODY WHO IS DYING?

Let us flesh out the principles we have been talking about with some illustrations of how such conversations can be constructed in practice. One gentleman I (Lorraine) spoke with years ago expressed hesitancy about dying. Ron would say that he still felt he had years left in him and that there were things he still wanted to do. He was very concerned about the effect of his possible absence on his two children, aged 16 and 19. We spoke over many months, as he sorted what it meant to be dying from pancreatic cancer at 56 years of age. This was not the death that Ron had planned for his life. He told me of regrets he had that his life would end at a young age. He felt as though he had "wasted his years" being caught up in alcohol and drugs, even though he and his wife had not had anything to do with drugs or alcohol for 15 years.

Ron did not appear to many people to be a deep thinker. He had spent the previous 15 years driving a truck and working as a landscaper. Both these professions suited his shy personality, because, as he worked, he could get lost in thought and not worry about too much social interaction. Once, he had said that he felt like a failure because he was no better than Walter Mitty—the Thurber character who was always swept away in fantasy rather than focusing on what he was doing in life (Thurber, 1931). Ron eloquently described how he had lived in fantasy, and harshly judged himself for this. Other people may have spoken of him as living in "denial," but I kept wondering how such a man could think of this as failure. He had overcome difficult circumstances and had maintained a strong marriage. And now he was facing death with courage.

Ron expressed many concerns about what his death might mean to his children. He knew that his wife would continue to be there for them, but was concerned about how things might be "without a man around the house." He was particularly concerned about his 16-year-old son. A few months earlier, his son had been arrested at a friend's party and charged with drinking under age and possession of marijuana. Without Ron's physical presence, he feared that drug use might worsen his son's trajectory into a place that Ron did not want him to go.

I spoke about this initially with only Ron and his wife, Darlene, present. Later, we included their children. I wanted to know about his hopes for the children. What did he hope they would do with their lives? What lessons had he hoped to impart to them, regardless of whether he was living or not? Many of Ron's answers were what most parents would hope for their children. He wanted them to be free from struggles, to find a good partner, and be content. I asked questions to explore how Ron's legacy might be included in their family and how he wanted to be remembered.

"What would you want them to know about your own struggles?"

"What would you hope your life legacies would mean to them?"

"How could your children use what you have learned about the effects of drugs and alcohol to benefit their own lives?"

"If you are not here physically to remind them, who else will bring to life your words and stories for their benefit?"

"Darlene, how do you imagine that you will stay connected with Ron's presence and stories when he is not here physically? How will this happen for your kids?"

"Which stories do you think will be the most beneficial for your children to remember about you and your life?"

Ron spoke at great length about these things. He acknowledged that he hadn't been "around" much for his kids. He had been out in bars and drinking for the first part of their lives. There had been times when he had thought he should have been dead following week-long binges of alcohol and drug use. He wanted his kids to know what it had meant to stop all this—for 15 years he had faced each day without drugs or alcohol.

"I want them to know how the preciousness of life can be wasted if they follow in my footsteps. I already see my son stepping into dangerous territory."

"How will he hold close your knowledge for the years ahead?" I asked.

Ron lit a cigarette and thought long about this. "I will have to tell him these things before I die. I am hoping that Darlene will keep these reminders around for the kids. She was there all the way and knows. She knows what it took for me to get sober and what it felt like to almost lose me. I want her to tell the kids to not go there like I did. I want her to keep telling them, 'Your Dad wouldn't want this.' I know she will do that for us."

COMFORTING CONVERSATIONS

These conversations were extremely important for Ron and his family. He gave his family advice about how he hoped they would live and choices he hoped they would make. He spoke about how he could assist them financially after he died and his wish that they would use these funds to move closer to their childhood communities. He spoke specifically and very firmly with his son about not using drugs. Following this conversation, his son attended a six-week counseling program for teens to promote a drug- and alcohol-free lifestyle. By talking directly about aspects that Ron wanted remembered from his life, he was able both to see an immediate impact on his family and to hope for a long-term positive impact.

In these conversations, we rehearsed many aspects of Ron's life with his family. They became an important audience for him in the process of making meaning of both his life and his death. We explored how family members would know that they were carrying his voice forward. We speculated about how he would like them to see him as a person of courage, and how he rose to the occasion in the face of death.

As part of remembering, it was also important for Ron to build a strong connection with his son. We fleshed out how he could be an important ongoing resource for his son, even after he was dead. I asked him about the story that his son did not know about who he was as a father. Many of Ron's answers were about how he decided to finally stop drinking and using drugs. It was important that he impart this information, in the hope that his son would inherit this sober legacy.

Ron shared with his children his Walter Mitty analogy that we had previously spoken of.

"I want you kids to not let things go by unnoticed and miss out," he said. "Too much of my life has been missed—I got caught up in unimportant things. I forgot that the most important thing is right here in this room with my family."

This family was not without difficulties. Remembering practices are not only about bringing forward the nice, easy parts of relationships. We were able to use their stories of challenge and hardship as resources for strength and future connection. As Ron consciously entrusted his wife with the legacy of his stories, he himself was reassured that the lessons of his own courage would be kept alive for his family's benefit.

ANTICIPATING WHAT WILL
BE REMEMBERED

What could also change at this point was Ron's story of his own life. The stories that are the stuff of memory are always selections from among many choices. What we remember is not fixed or static. The meanings of stories are always fluid and up for debate. The dominant stories by which Ron had been making sense of his own life had constructed his approaching death as a waste. These stories had convinced him that he only had 15 years of good life—the years after his drinking ended.

As practices of remembering continued to develop, those 15 years could grow into 20, 30, 50, and more. In this way, the lessons of life need not die with a person but can be carried forward in ways that serve the next generation and their children.

Ron had been concerned that the knowledge he had gained in changing his relationship with drugs and alcohol would die along with him. Over a few sessions, I explored with him what it would look like if this knowledge were not to die. What would have to happen if Ron's presence were to remain at least as important in the family as it was at that moment? Perhaps his influence might grow even stronger.

This process of actively constructing what will be remembered can begin well before a person dies. Remembering conversations are about more than just planning one's own memorial or selecting which hymns are to be played at a funeral. They can be about asking persons who are dying to select out highlights of life that are worth preserving in memory and ritual observance. The dying person can chart the course of remembering that her or his loved ones will navigate. Participation in conversations before death, not about what will be lost but about what will be remembered, can actually be very heartening and uplifting for the dying person. Such conversations can offer solace in the face of apprehensive or fearful aspects of death. It makes a difference to know that we matter. Often, the more precise and detailed the conversations that convey this information, the more comforting they are.

As professionals, we can invite loved ones to specify in the presence of the dying person how they will continue to include their loved one in conversation in ways that affirm that the life of the dying person does matter, and will continue to matter. Such conversations can communicate, and even grow, enormous respect. They can even make this time before death an occasion for learning as the dying person comes to appreciate more fully that their lives—that all our lives—are not inconsequential.

The effect of these conversations may be the production of comforting thoughts that enable everyone, including the dying person, to face death, knowing that what has been important about their life will continue even after the end of their bodily existence. This effect is not the conventional production of grief. It does not focus on the acceptance of painful feelings of loss. These may well be present. However, we would question the usefulness of the conventional emphasis on encouraging the emotional expression of such pain. This emphasis tends unnecessarily to select out what is painful from what may be more comforting. Remembering conversations do the opposite. They select for emphasis what can provide emotional sustenance through the transition to death.

CHOOSING OUR REMEMBERING AUDIENCES

One decision that came from the conversations with Ron and Darlene was to involve Ron's sister in the process. She, too, had come through challenges in her life with alcohol and, like her brother, was no longer committed to alcohol's limited vision for her life. Ron and Darlene asked Marissa to help keep Ron's knowledge around for his children—"to kind of act like a godmother" for them. We also decided that Marissa would assist Darlene in not being the only adult carrying Ron's membership card in her wallet. For Ron, it was very comforting to add her to the audience for his desire to be remembered. It was a comfort that was accented further by his spiritual belief that what mattered was here on this earth, not in a world after.

In these ways, Ron was playing a part in the choice of who would carry his memory forward, rather than leaving this up to chance or in the hands of others. He was also leaving both Darlene and Marissa the legacy of a conversational context in which his memory might live. The chances were increased that they would talk together about his legacy and that this would make it easier for both of them to remember him.

When we acknowledge that our relationships never die, only our physical bodies do, we are honoring another's spirit, their story, their connection to us, and the relationship we share with them. We can bring forward the best of our shared pasts into shaping the story of our future relationship. The kinds of questions used in "appreciative inquiry" (Hammond, 1996) perform a similar function to what we are talking about here. We have an opportunity before someone dies to reflect and review, and even revise, stories of this person's past to be carried into the future. We might be curious of someone who is dying to know what stories they want told after their death. We might also inquire about what connections they hope that others might develop after their death. We might ask who the dying person would commission as the keepers of their stories.

RITUALS OF REMEMBERING

Another type of practice that builds ongoing membership and connection is the continuing of rituals that were important to the person while alive. One family mentioned how the children take turns filling the bird feeders in the yard that were important to their mother. Each time they complete this otherwise simple task, they are affirming something that was valuable to their mother in her life and honoring the commitment they made prior to her death.

Often too, families create new practices to honor their loved one or combine aspects of old and new to create rituals. A woman sent an excerpt she had written in her church newsletter two years after the death of her husband.

> I often bring flowers from my husband's Phil's beloved garden to place on his memorial stone in the columbarium. On Easter, I was so pleased to hear the delighted squeals of the children as they hid and hunted for eggs throughout the garden. One child asked me what I was doing and I told her. She thought for a moment, then asked if it was OK if they hid eggs in the foliage behind the stone. I said I thought it was a wonderful idea! To me, the columbarium should always be a place full of life and laughter, as well as a place for contemplation and serenity. It is so important that those we love and have gone before us are still a vital part of the whole picture.

We encourage people to speak candidly to the person who is dying about the ritual practices they will continue to uphold. Rituals are important. They organize pausing moments that thicken the significance of relationships within families and communities. Rituals can develop over a lifetime, or be introduced by the person who is dying before death.

"Will you go out for a meal on my birthday and think of me after I die?" my mother (John) asked me 18 months before her death.

As she neared the end of her life, it was comforting to her to think that her birthday would not cease to be celebrated after she had died. Since we commonly have rituals of remembering for the living around birthdays, it made sense for her to ask that we extend this after her death.

TELLING THE STORY OF DEATH

It can also be of value to talk with persons who are dying about how they would like to be talked about in the future. If we recall that how we story our experience shapes our present and future choices, then speaking about these variations is more than just an exercise in the language arts. For example, we might want to speak with a person who is dying about how they want the story of their death recounted.

"What do you want your loved ones to say about how you approached death?"

This question opens up reflexive space to help people shape their actions. Responses to this question can increase the range of available choices. What's more, hope is embedded within the future orientation of this question. It asks a dying person to look to the future. Pride too can be a product of such conversations.

We might ask, "What aspects of the way you have handled your illness will you want your loved ones to be proud of?"

"How do you want the last part of your life to be recalled?"

"How do you hope that the story of your death might help your loved ones when it is their turn to die? What lessons might there be for them here?"

"How might you want your story told to the generations yet to come?"

These questions invite the telling of stories of identity that feature qualities like courage and strength. Such stories are often remembered vividly by family members, simply because they get talked about with friends and family often in the days that follow.

GROWING MEMBERSHIP ACROSS
GENERATIONS

Many years ago now, I (Lorraine) met one family who faced an extremely hard challenge. When we met in their home, the doctor had only told them the day earlier, "There is nothing more that can be done." This was a far different reality from the hopeful path of chemotherapy, radiation, and a medical cure they had been on only a week beforehand. Her health had been destroyed by a cancer that had been eating away at her body for the past two years. Surrounding this woman of 50 years was her loving family, a committed and heart-broken husband, their three young adult children, and the dying woman's brother. Even though she was still able to converse with me and speak clearly, I could see from her physical condition that death was not far away.

Initially, we spoke about how the information that "no further treatment was possible" was such a leap for them when they were expecting something very different. They certainly were not expecting consultation with hospice workers. The changes required them to turn on a dime. As they struggled with this, I asked them, not about what was sad in this, but about what now they would hope for.

I wanted to know, "With this dramatic change in plans, knowing what is occurring and the choices before you, what do you want? For example, where do you want to die and who do you want to be with you now and for the next period of time?"

In raising these issues, I do not believe I was callously ignoring the seriousness of the shock. I was, however, inviting them to take on a measure of control in what appeared to be an out-of-control situation. We explored some stories about her connections with her family through these questions.

I wanted to expand a conversation of hope in the face of difficulty. So we spoke about how her stories might be carried forward.

How did she want her family telling the story of her dying? What did she hope they would remember years down the road? How would she want to stay connected to her children? How might they form a stronger relationship with her over the years? What would she like them to be telling one another that she would say during challenges that they might face ahead? What pearls of information about her should her husband keep close for them, as well as for others in their extended family and community?

She began to tell us the start of the stories that she wanted to be remembered on her behalf. She wanted them to know how much she loved them. She spoke about how her children had meant the world to her and how being a mother brought her great joy. She spoke about her strong connection with her husband, in his presence, and how much she had enjoyed being his partner for 32 years. Yes, she wished it could be longer, but she also was now aware of the gratitude for these years too. She was mapping out the aspects of her life that she wanted others to take note of—the parts she and her family felt were of substance.

In her presence, the children also spoke. Through many tears, we talked about how they would in fact be living her legacy. They talked about their plans to finish college in honor of her and what their hopes were for their careers. They both spoke about how they would like to have children someday and to tell them the stories of their grandmother. Prior to dying, this woman had the chance to hear their plans to keep their mother's love close to them.

I asked them about how they would be introducing their yet unborn children to their grandmother in future years. What were their hopes about how their children would come to know about their grandmother's impact and influence in their family over time?

All had the chance to tell these stories of intergenerational significance. They spoke about the lessons of love that she had taught them and that they planned to impart to their children. All had the chance to reflect and speak about how she mattered.

These conversations affirm connection, even in the face of death. For the person who is dying, these conversations can ease the fear of death. The approach of death has less power to undermine the meaning of a person's life, if that meaning has been located in significant relationships that will continue on. The foregrounding of what carries on, and the backgrounding of what is lost, makes a difference to the period before death. It facilitates conversation about death itself. Somehow it becomes less unspeakable. Instead, it becomes a context for the discussion of life, as it has been, and as it will continue on. If relationship continues over time and traverses the physical reality of death, as we believe, then to speak a final good-bye is never needed.

CHAPTER SIX

How Can We Stay Close?

> I feel very strongly (and I am not alone in this) that some good comes from the dead to the living in the months or weeks after the death . . . Certainly they often seem just at that time to be very near us.
>
> *C. S. Lewis to Miss Vera Matthews on the death of her father, 27 March 1951* (Harding & Dyson, 1981, p. 163)*

When a person dies, there is a period of transition for relationships that begins. In this chapter, we want to consider the impact of the transition for those who are still living. We also want to spell out some ways of speaking with people that might assist in the process of negotiating this transition. We are interested in what makes this transition easier and less painful, rather than harder or more painful. If we start from the premise that death does not equate with the end of a relationship, then our task becomes discovering the ways in which a relationship might live on. The challenge for those whose loved one has died is how to stay close, rather than how to suffer the absence of the person who has died.

AVOIDING A FOCUS ON LOSS

Conventional approaches to grief have tended to focus the attention of those who are grieving on what they have lost when someone dies rather than on what is not lost. Such approaches are based on an emphasis on the "realistic" view that, in the end, we lose all our relationships, attachments, and possessions. We think even this assumption can be challenged. It is an assumption founded on a possessive view of relationship with the world. We might, for example, take a different stance if we view attachments from a decentered perspective in which the individual is not placed in such a central focus.

---

*From *A Book of Condolences: Classic Letters of Bereavement,* edited by Rachel Harding and Mary Dyson, © 1981 by the editors. Reprinted by permission of The Continuum Publishing Group.

From this perspective, the communities to which we belong, the projects we hold dear, the network of relationships in which we take part will continue on and not be lost when we die. Our contributions to them will be taken up by others and added to. If we keep this focus in mind, death does not have to end the individual possession of our meaning in the world. Death takes its place more as a moment of transition in the ongoing process of life of which we play a part.

A brief story illustrates this point. When we were traveling together through England, we took some time to attend an evensong in the magnificent cathedral in Durham. It was a sung evensong and was a beautiful event to experience. In explanation of the evensong, the clergyman who was leading the service invited us to hear the song as part of an ongoing conversation between God and his people that had been happening for centuries all around the world. We were stepping into the conversation for a brief moment as many had done long before us and would continue to do so long after we are dead.

In New Zealand, I (John) am familiar with a Maori perspective that punctuates life in a similar way. From a Maori perspective, children are born into a *whanau* (roughly translatable as an extended family), rather than to individual parents. They go through life and eventually die, but are never lost to their *whanau,* which carries on through the generations. There are many Maori ritual practices designed to remind us to remember the dead in the context of an ongoing conversation within a community that is not reliant on their embodied presence.

These are both cultural meanings that point us toward a view of life that does not privilege the individual as in possession of relationships, identities, projects, and objects. Instead, this view invites us to consider our lives as visited by relationships, identities, projects, and objects. We are but temporary partakers of the opportunity of life in relation to them. From this perspective, loss has a different meaning. Our attachments are more ephemeral and less essential to our being. Our experiences of loss may be correspondingly less wrenching. They can be incorporated more smoothly into the context of the continuity of community, of projects, and of cultural meanings.

If we emphasize only the "realistic" assumption of loss, what carries on can be neglected. We are commonly invited into places that immediately cut us off from the memory of our loved one. People want to know if we had a chance to "say good-bye," or to talk about "unfinished business." People ask if our loved one's death was expected or not. We are told that, even though we are sad now, in time we will get over the pain and get on with things. We are often encouraged to "keep busy and keep our minds off things." We might be simultaneously encouraged to feel the loss keenly in order to reach a place where the pain starts to subside and the reality of death is accepted. If we are unlucky enough to receive therapeutic attention, in the name of "grief work," that focuses on the "reality of loss" and constantly revisits the impact of death, we might actually increase our level of suffering.

We are not convinced that this orientation is helpful. Stroebe and Schut (2001) state it bluntly:

> . . . we suggest that ruminating about a loss will worsen grief and depression . . . (p. 65).

A focus on loss privileges only part of the reality of negotiating bereavement. In the very process of emphasizing what is lost or does not continue, what does not have to be lost or what can continue is de-emphasized. Hence, when people are helped to accept the "reality" of loss, the other reality of continuing relationship is not given enough room for development. As a result, many stories that are not about loss at all are neglected. For example, in the rush to speak about loss, stories can be left untold about how a family may be proud of what has transpired. Emotional expression of things like appreciation or joy or loving commitment can be overlooked in favor of the expression of feelings of sadness and loss. Stories of the benefits of what death might bring can be brought forward too.

I (Lorraine) had a conversation with a young woman whose husband had died only a month before. She told me she was feeling guilty that she was mad at him. She was tired from getting up at night to take care of their young child and she was mad he was not there to help.

I asked her whether she thought he would be helpful if he were there physically.

"No," she said, "He was a heavy sleeper and would sleep through the children's nighttime crying." She laughed at this and said she would be mad at him whether he was dead or alive this week.

From this perspective, we were able to explore the relationship's continuity. We discussed how she was still experiencing a full range of emotion in this relationship, just as we often do in partnership. She was still very much involved with her dead husband but had come to think that because he was dead she should no longer be mad at him. Somehow, her expressing this irritation with him invited her into feeling so guilty that she was dishonoring her connection with him. When she spoke about her consistency and her continued connection, her story expanded.

"You mean I don't have to just be sad?" she asked.

We do not believe that the emphasis on loss is the most comforting emphasis in conversations with the bereaved. This is not to deny the presence or the impact of loss. But we do think it is important to at least balance this with an emphasis on what continues on, what does not die with the death of a body. Moreover, we have also had sufficient experience of such conversations to believe that they provide more of a sense of comfort than an emphasis on loss produces. In this way, they help people negotiate the relational transitions of death more smoothly than a more wrenching emphasis on "facing the loss" might offer.

WHAT BENEFITS DOES DEATH BRING?

Gordon had just signed on to a hospice program and was doing fairly well physically. He was eating and getting around without problem and was mainly free from discomfort. At 65, he and his wife Rachel had many wonderful experiences to reflect on from their 23 years of marriage. In spite of his terminal diagnosis, Gordon was full of life and funny stories. He welcomed visitors with open arms and a positive upbeat demeanor.

When we spoke, we all imagined that he still had a good couple of months ahead in which he could enjoy his family and friends. I (Lorraine) asked him how he wanted to use the time in the best possible way.

He responded, "There is nothing left I need to do. Sure, I like the time, but I have done what I need to in my life. Had great kids and a great wife and fished and hunted. It couldn't have been better."

He explained that people were free to give him advice about how they might use their final days to travel exotic lands or purchase special items.

"Nope," he said. "Already done all those things."

When Gordon suddenly died a week later, we all were caught off guard. I was concerned about what this might mean for his wife. Would she feel cheated out of time they were still planning on?

I spoke with her the day after his death. Rather than focusing on the experience of loss, I was curious about whether there were stories that could affirm the obvious love they had for one another.

Rachel told me that Gordon had become ill and had started throwing up a little blood. Hearing noises, she went to check on him. She could see he was woozy and knelt down in front of him. He fainted into her arms and died.

I asked her, "If Gordon were here and able to comment on his death, what might he say?"

"He'd be pleased. He didn't want to suffer."

"Do you think he would be happy that he died in your arms?"

"I don't think he wanted it any other way. He told a few people how he did not want to have to take a lot of medicine or have pain. He died before any of that."

"Gordon told me you were tough last week and, in spite of his concerns for you, he knew you could handle this. What do you think he'd be saying about how you're doing so far?"

"The same. He'd say that I was tough still. He used to say I was his life. That when we met, his life wasn't going very well, and that I gave him a new lease on life."

"Do you think he had a confidence that you would do all right, then, with how his death happened sooner than we thought?"

"He did. He just knew I could handle this."

"Rachel, what might he say if he was to offer us an opinion about how he died sooner, rather than later? Do you think he might say there were advantages, or disadvantages, or perhaps no difference?"

"He definitely would say it was an advantage to die the way he did. He didn't want to suffer or to lose the ability to take care of his own needs."

"Really! In spite of this being hard for you, he'd say this was an advantage to have died when and how he did."

"Yes, definitely. Everything kind of fell into place. It is strange. Everybody was able to get a plane here, or talk with him recently, and it all just fell into place."

This conversation was important for Rachel. We could have quite easily focused on stories of loss and missing. She had had the wind knocked out of her by the way that Gordon died. However, to speak about all that she had lost would not serve to invite ongoing membership or relationship. Developing these stories would potentially magnify beliefs that would not be immediately helpful.

Instead, we spoke about the benefits of his death. It was not that we wanted to hurry his going or to adopt a cavalier attitude of, "Thank God, that's done with." We wanted to highlight aspects of the events that would demonstrate pride, love, and strength in a challenging circumstance. In this conversation, Rachel created the beginnings of a story that would profoundly connect them for the rest of her days. It was a comforting story more than a wrenching or painful one.

When we look at possible benefits that come from death, we can create stories focused on themes other than loss. Research supports the idea that fostering stories of hardship and loss does not produce more effective processing of bereavement. In fact, more and more studies are re-examining the assumptions of grief. In one detailed study, Frantz, Farrell, and Trolley (2001) describe factors that shape positive outcomes during bereavement. Eighty-four percent of respondents they interviewed indicated that positive outcomes had occurred following death. Included were reports of increased closeness within families and relationships, greater appreciation of life, increased patience and personal strength, relief at the end of suffering for a loved one, and a decrease in fear of death.

Death can invite many stories to unfold. Our interest remains in stories that affirm connection and membership after the death of a loved one. Rachel's and Gordon's story affirmed a love story for their current community and for the communities who had yet to know them. All who hear these stories can become beneficiaries of their love when we weave these threads into rich fabric.

Here is another extract from a counseling conversation in which a woman recalls, some years after her mother's death, a moment of closeness that has been sustaining for their relationship since her death.

Justine: I think in many ways she tried to make it better.

John: She tried in little ways to get around oppression?

Justine: Yeah she tried very hard to get around it. I mean oppression was alcoholism. It was the guiding thing in our family. . . . There are things about Mum I treasure . . .

John: Tell me what you treasure . . . now.

Justine: I still remember one particular day. Just walking home from school with her. She used to wait for me and we would walk home together. And just one particular lovely autumn day. Just walking down the road with my Mum, that's all . . . and just feeling everything was OK. . . . Quite often, when everyone would go to bed at night she and I would sit up and talk. She could talk and tell stories, but you couldn't while Dad was around.

REINCORPORATING MEMBERSHIP

After someone dies, the relationship between the living person and the dead person does not need to end but it cannot continue in the form that it has previously. But this is a different thing from saying that it is finished. Barbara Myerhoff and Michael White have suggested that negotiating this transition involves a "reincorporation" of a person's membership in their loved ones' lives in new ways. These ways place new requirements on those who continue to live. They are required, for example, to carry on a person's voice in their memories, rather than hearing it out loud.

We can assist people going through this process of reincorporation by asking questions that invite the continuance of relationship in new forms. As Rachel and I talked, I asked questions to thicken the story of her relationship with her husband. She began to give details about how he had come to see her as strong, and how he knew she would manage through the time of transition. She was continuing his voice and his story about her in these ways.

We further thickened these stories when his daughter Michele joined the discussion. They spoke about how they wanted his memorial service. Michele said that many people would come, as her father had been so well-liked.

"Would he like to have stories told about him at the service?" I asked.

"Yes. He would enjoy listening to all the stories about him—many I'm sure I even don't know."

"What might you learn about your Dad from his memorial? How do you think you'll know him better after his memorial than you know him now?"

"That would be great. I'd like to hear more about him with his friends too. He always had friends over here—people I never even met. It would be nice to hear from them. He could cuss up a storm. That will be part of the stories too, I suppose."

I told them that I knew this about Gordon. When we first met, he had told me what a "son-of-a-bitch" he was. We all laughed about how this was anything but true but he got a kick out of telling people this.

We were not overlooking the sadness present. Tears flowed freely as we spoke about what were Gordon's likes and hobbies and relationships. We were quickly building a new bridge between Gordon and the people he loved. The conversation was mixing the mortar that would hold the bricks of his memory together and would ensure that his presence would be still richly available to his family.

CONVERSING WITH DEAD LOVED ONES

As we invited ongoing membership for Gordon and his family, we opened the prospects of this connection strengthening over time. One of the many ways that people continue this is by talking directly to those who have died. People do not often talk about this for fear of being thought to be in denial, crazy, or worse. In spite of that, it is very common. Rachel broached this topic the day after Gordon died.

"How do you think he'd like the memorial you're planning?" I asked.

"I think he might like it. Guess I will have to tell him about it."

"Yes. I imagine so. Do you think you will have a lot of conversations with him?"

"Well I hadn't thought about it yet. You know my sister told me how she speaks with her husband all the time—just like he was there, but he's been dead for years now."

"Do you think she'd encourage you to do the same?"

"I guess she would, but I hadn't thought about it."

"I wonder what parts you might want to make sure Gordon knows about the memorial?"

"Oh, he would like to know what his friends might be saying about him. He always said that with him you get what you see."

Encouraging people to speak with their dead loved one is one way to explore ongoing membership. Often, these dialogues go on in our heads. We know exactly how a person would respond to most questions after years of cohabitation. We carry their voices and stories with us all the time. It can be a place of comfort and a resource to have continued access to their words and voices.

Two months later, I had the chance to catch up with Rachel on her birthday. I was curious about how her birthday would be different since Gordon's death.

"What did Gordon do for your birthdays in the past?" I inquired.

"Not too much. Sometimes we'd go out to eat, but a lot we'd just stay home. I've been meaning to talk to Gordon about this," Rachel laughed.

"So what are you going to do for your birthday?"

"I am going out to dinner with my sister," Rachel said.

"I guess you did talk to Gordon then. Since you got some action."

"Yeah. I told him that I'd take him along but that I would have to eat his cake for him."

If we keep relationships alive after death, there is a sense in which we not only get to have our cake and eat it, but to also have someone else's cake as well.

MAINTAINING AND DEVELOPING RELATIONSHIP

Just after the death of a person, family members are often at sea with a hundred details to attend to: people to notify, legal affairs to manage, memorials and funerals to plan and attend. These initial moments can feel overwhelming.

But there is also opportunity in this transition period. It is when new seedlings can be planted in a relationship. We are required to form a new relationship with a dead loved one, without their physical presence to assist us. We may have to work to re-establish this connection in the midst of a flurry of people and activities. Some events in this transition period may be remembered in detail and can be used for rich story development for years to come. However, in the midst of the overwhelmingness, it may not be easy to notice all the small plants springing up from the seedlings that we are planting. A focus for professional conversation, then, should be to nurture these seedlings, water them, and protect them from being trampled on.

One place of immediate opportunity for relational renewal is the funeral or memorial. When families are deciding what to include, we can actively encourage them to build in many opportunities for stories. As Janice Nadeau (2001) observes, "Most families run out of opportunities to tell stories before they run out of stories to tell" (p. 322). Stories connect the living with the dead, and with each other, and put flesh on the bones of relationship. Therefore, we often might wonder with a family:

> If you were to leave the funeral or memorialization with a much closer and richer understanding of your loved one, what might need to transpire?

Notice how this question assumes that the funeral will provide a chance to learn about the person and the network of relationships that she or he has been part of. Remembering is not just about what we already know. It is an organic process of growth and construction. Therefore, we can explore who else might hold interesting stories that expand our understanding. Even in the repetition of familiar stories, new meanings can develop (Nadeau, 2001). We also encourage families to create opportunities, besides the formal ritual, where further stories can be shared. Not everyone feels comfortable speaking in front of a crowd but many would be delighted to share a story over a meal.

One family created a beautiful ritual for their mother's memorial. At the gathering, they provided slender candles in beautiful and contrasting colors. People were invited to light a candle and to tell the story of their particular connection with her. As each candle was lit and laughter and tears were shared, the candles were placed in a large bowl of white sand and allowed to burn out. At the end of the memorial, there was an exquisite mosaic of melted wax in the sand. This woman's daughter was an artist. She took photos of the rich hues and colors left behind and commented, "Here's my mother in all her different colors."

A funeral can create a scaffold for building new stories from the old. Imagine this family as they light candles in the future to honor their mother. Each candle lighting can remind them of the richness created at the memorial and serve as a renewal of their connection with her. Occasionally, some families may choose not to have any formal gathering and may look to create rituals of remembrance that are personal and private. Conversely, a family may have more than one funeral for a deceased loved one in separate locations to honor various people who have been involved with the deceased. There may be different services for people whose clubs were separated by lifestyle choices. There are no rules for what is appropriate or required when memorializing a loved one. What is important is to affirm connection and to open possibility for future membership in our club of life.

RITUALS FOR REMEMBERING

Often people create rituals around the spreading of a person's ashes after cremation. The spreading of ashes is a ritual that can be co-opted for remembering purposes. My family (John) spread my mother's ashes on her birthday around the site where her wedding photos had been taken 49 years earlier.

Sometimes, the anniversary of the death can become a day for remembering rituals that celebrate the life of a dead loved one and seek to incorporate this life into ongoing family traditions. Or Father's Day might become a focus for remembering a dead father. One family did this by taking a family hike on this day (Tiller, 2002). Another widow celebrated Christmas with her dead husband by decorating the urn that contained his ashes with Christmas decorations that he had loved during his life (Tiller, 2002).

Quilting is a tradition that lends itself to remembering. One woman showed me (Lorraine) a quilt she had made out of panels cut from her dead husband's tee-shirts. Others express their desire to remember in a written mode. They might write personal stories or keep a journal in which they conduct conversations with themselves or with their dead loved one (Neimeyer, 2002; Pennebaker, 2000).

Remembering rituals can also be simple, personal, and private moments involving regular practices. I (John) have used my dead daughter's name as a password in some contexts that serve to remind me of her presence in my life on a daily basis. Sometimes people make it a regular habit to spend a few minutes of each day, or each week, remembering the significance of a loved one in their lives. Perhaps they might mark these moments by the burning of a candle or by watering a garden.

Such rituals incorporate memories of the past into the present and make links with what we want to sustain into the future. They mark the meanings we are making and they underscore our sense of what is significant and who is important to us. They dramatize through enactment the claims we make about such meanings and render the truths around which we seek to perform identification visible to other people (Myerhoff, 1982). They help us negotiate the transitions that death requires and can serve many purposes, including "healing, supporting, comforting, transitioning, guiding, reconciling, sustaining and sharing" (Tiller, 2002, p. 343).

All of these remembering practices make it possible for us to make sense of death, not so much as an end to life, but as a transition. As with other life transitions, there are different ways of going about it. There are culturally prescribed practices that give shape to how we experience it. And there are poetically unique elements to any single experience of death. Remembering practices can enhance our appreciation of the developmental possibilities of death (Bird & Drewery, 2000). In other words, death affords us the chance to make the most of life, even after we have left behind the act of breathing. And remembering practices enhance the likelihood that we can make the most of these possibilities, just as works of art, music, or poetry enhance what we can envision, or resonate with, or speak into being.

CHAPTER SEVEN
Keeping a Plate Set for Grandma

> It is true, I think, that they only seem to have gone, for that lovely store of golden years which you made together—years of life well lived, full of delightful interests shared and lovely pleasant things, is really as much with you now as say last month—last year— anytime.
>
> *Rex Whistler to Mrs. Belloc-Lowndes on the death of her husband, 28 March 1940* (Harding & Dyson, 1981, p. 166)*

We have talked about the meaning of death for those who are dying, as well as for their loved ones immediately after a death. Now, we shall turn our attention to the development of remembering over time. If membership does not end with death, then neither is the relationship with the dead person frozen in the events of the past. Remembering is not therefore only about revisiting memories of the dead person's life. It can take on a much more creative dimension as we continue to incorporate a person's membership in the events and rituals of a lifetime, and it can continue as we hand stories down through the generations. This chapter will address how remembering conversations can continue to grow and unfold a person's membership and even allow it to take on new significant meanings 10, 20, or 50 years after a person has died.

An exclusive focus on what is lost invites us to locate our relationship with a dead loved one only in the past, when they were alive in body. However, after someone dies our lives continue to unfold. We take on new identities, enter different life phases, and bring new people into membership in our clubs. The challenge of remembering conversation now moves beyond the task of incorporating memories and

*From *A Book of Condolences: Classic Letters of Bereavement,* edited by Rachel Harding and Mary Dyson, © 1981 by the editors. Reprinted by permission of The Continuum Publishing Group.

echoes of previous conversations with the deceased into our consciousness. It takes on a developmental focus to braid the posthumous
with the living. Perhaps, we might introduce a dead grandmother to her
newborn grandchildren and express the joy that she would share in the
prospect of their lives. We might speculate about the meaning to her of
events in the life of a family. We might consult her opinion on parenting
in ways that we never had cause to while she was alive. In these ways,
we might continue to populate our conversations with her voice and
our consciousness with a richer range of voices than if we stuck rigidly
to the voices of the real in the present. In these ways, she might continue
to live on in her stories and even augment them along the way. Let
us look at some examples of remembering conversations that take
on this dimension.

WEAVING THE DEAD INTO ONGOING
STORIES OF LIFE

Family conversations often evolve around social rituals, both small
and large. The challenge for remembering lies in finding ways to include
the dead in these conversations. Here is one story about a family who
found a creative way to do this.

One of the families I (Lorraine) worked with was very much in love
with their father/grandfather. They adored him as a kind and living
presence for all of them. Whenever they had a question or problem,
they knew that they could come to him and he would patiently listen.
He was a leader in his family and in his community, as well having
been an influential medical practitioner and was strongly committed
to a legacy of civic responsibility.

After he died during the month of November, his family struggled
with how they were going to continue to have his presence with him
over the upcoming Christmas holiday. As I spoke with four of his
children, their house was already filled with decorations of the season.
I asked them about this. They explained that their father always
loved Christmas, particularly as it meant special time for family
gatherings. Traditionally, they would have him "play Santa" and dress
up in a Santa suit to hand out presents on Christmas Eve. They feared
that this Christmas would be too painful to continue with some of
the joys that previous years had brought.

They told me how the Christmas stockings were always a lovely
family time. He particularly loved watching the children find the
small presents, candies, and money that he hid for them deep in the
stockings.

I inquired if they were going to hang his stocking alongside the others this year. Did they think he would still like to have his stocking hung up?

They spoke about this possibility and, as they did so, a wonderful thought grew. They started to tell many of the stories connected with Christmases gone by. What if they were to record these stories? They decided they could make a few notes and place them in his stocking hanging by the fireplace.

Christmas Eve rolled around and they all gathered just as they had done for years. After the smaller children had unwrapped their stocking stuffers, they sat down to dinner. Slowly, the family began to pull from this kind man's stocking, all the little slips of paper and notes of stories that they each had contributed with precious reminders written on them. As each was read aloud during dinner, more stories began to grow about their connection with their father and grandfather.

The second year following his death, Christmas came around again. In the mail I received a note from this man's wife. "We are well set up for Christmas with the kids and grandkids doing most of it. I have a little red votive candle in the nice little holder that you gave me last year. . . . His Christmas stocking is still at the head of the line with last year's notes still in it, and we'll add more this year. Don't know how many years we will keep that up, but it works for now."

NOT "GETTING OVER IT"

When a person dies, they do not cease to be the same person they have always been to us. They still are our spouse, parent, child, friend, or co-worker. In this regard, their membered title does not change status. If our goal is to "get back to normal" or to "get over" a person's death, we are expecting ourselves to perform, to some degree, an act of erasure. What makes it painful is that we often find we cannot erase that they once were right beside us. We cannot delete shared memories, or gloss over the significance they had in our lives.

What we find consistently when we talk with people is that, even though a death may have occurred years previously, their loved one is still a part of their lives. People who have had children die commonly speak of this. In fact, people whose loved one has been dead for many years often speak about how the connection has grown after 5, 10, or 30 years following their deaths. Bev Gatenby (1998) solicited many such stories from parents whose children had died. She speaks both to the particular experience of grief following the death of a child and to the long lasting connection that continues to live on.

> . . . parents continue to live out a bond with their child. Marie comments, "I'd have grown with her if she were still alive and I've grown and changed with her after she died too (p. 127).

I (John) had an experience that I found powerfully instructive in this regard, after my daughter died. Julia had been dead for several months, several anguished months, when Christine and I, in something of a restless state, left our life in New Zealand and traveled to Britain. We toured around England and Scotland and it was in Scotland that we met up with a couple who were in their seventies. They were the parents of a friend whom we knew in New Zealand. They were very hospitable and looked after us and showed us around for three days.

On the evening before we were due to leave them, I asked whether they had known about our daughter's death and explained how this had been part of why we were there. Until then, we had not spoken about this. They said that their daughter had written and told them about Julia's death. Then the husband said that this had been an important reason why they had wanted to have us stay. At this point, his eyes misted up and he announced that they had had a daughter who had died 40 years previously. As he shared this, his wife was overcome with tears and felt that she had to leave the room, as he continued to explain about their daughter's death.

My experience at this moment was of being profoundly touched. In a way that I did not fully understand at the time, I was enormously relieved to hear this story and to see that these two were still emotionally affected by their daughter's death, even 40 years later. It was as if she was still very present in their lives. The relief I experienced I later described to myself as being encouraged by this example that I did not have to expunge Julia from my life. If these people could still feel keenly their daughter's presence in their hearts many years later, then so could I. This idea was more comforting than anything else I was offered at that time. In the midst of a strong sense of loss, I was offered a story of what was not lost but had stayed very much alive. If I could imagine that, in 40 years time, I could still have Julia's presence in my life, affecting my relations with other people, then her death was less wrenching and terrible to bear.

It is now more than 20 years since Julia's death and this knowledge of her ongoing significance is much more secure. I know that she has not only stayed alive inside me but that she has helped me to make connections with many other people, just as this couple's daughter was continuing to do through enabling their connection with us. I have particularly appreciated how Julia has introduced me to other people who have experienced the death of a child and enabled me to do what this couple did for me. In this sense, her significance in my life is not frozen at the point of her death. It continues to be added to in new conversations and she gets introduced to new people in my life. At this very moment of writing, imagining who might be reading these words and having thoughts and responses enhances the significance of Julia's existence. I find this now more than just comforting. It has become a source of joy. As long as such events keep occurring, in a very tangible way, Julia continues to live as a member in my club of life. Her membership is active too in the conversations in which she takes part.

DELIBERATELY KEEPING MEMORY ALIVE

We believe it to be helpful for professionals to actively encourage families to incorporate stories of their loved one in their conversations, to continue invoking their memory and presence through ritual, and to enlarge the communities in which their stories are told. This can be achieved through the re-creation of rituals that a family shared with the deceased and/or through the growing of rituals over time in honor of the deceased. The celebrations and rituals may be elaborate, such as a yearly birthday party, or they may be quiet acts that affirm the connection. The following is an example of the latter.

An elderly woman told us about her conversations with her son. She explained that she speaks with him daily. Each morning, while tidying her house for her daily events, she tells her son about her life and about what she has planned for the day. As she sweeps the floors and starts the laundry, she takes 10 or 15 minutes to converse with him. Even though his death came more than 15 years previously, this ritual ensures that their connection is never forgotten.

Here is an excerpt from a counseling conversation in which a woman is remembering her mother who died 10 years previously. In the process she is making meaning of events in her own life in relation to her mother's perspective on it.

John: I'm interested that she felt guilty because in guilt there's a sense of aspiration for something better.

Justine: Yeah, she wanted me to have what she never had . . . to be. . . . She was proud of the fact that I wanted to be a teacher. She really was.

John: What was she proud of?

Justine: Well someone going to university from our family was unheard of! She would have been enormously proud now.

John: What would she say now about you and the work that you do?

Justine: She would have just glowed and my grandmother would have too. My grandmother was my refuge.

John: So your Mum would just glow if she could see you now. What would she be glowing about?

Justine: Oh it would be about that I have achieved what I have academically. That I have a career. And you know what I think she would be really proud of . . . that I left Garth.

John: Because she couldn't do that?

Justine: Because she would never leave Dad. I think she would have been quite jealous that I managed to get free.

In this kind of conversation, each new event in life offers further opportunity for new remembering if we ask the question about what it would mean to a dead loved one.

I (John) had a conversation with my father some 12 months after my mother died. My father had come to stay with me for 10 days. Before he was to return home, he announced that he wanted to take us out for a meal.

I protested that he did not have to do that and said that I would be happy to take him out for a meal.

"No," he insisted. "If Mum was here, this is what she would want to do. And she would never forgive me if I didn't do this."

We laughed and I understood his intent. I replied, "Well, I am glad to hear that you're still answerable to her."

Answerability or addressivity is a concept that Bakhtin (1986) stresses in his notion of dialogue. It refers to the extent to which the person(s) we are speaking to is/are already shaping our words before we utter them as we anticipate their response. It also refers to the extent to which we are always speaking in response to others' utterances, never in any completely original context. Any utterance therefore needs to be understood in terms of this quality of addressivity. This idea is a basic building block in Bakhtin's theory of discourse. An implication of it is that even after death we can shape the utterances of the living as they construct meaning in answer to remembered utterances of dead persons.

INTRODUCING THE DEAD TO NEW MEMBERS

I (Lorraine) have a 10-year-old daughter, Addison, who speaks often about her grandmother. She speaks about their relationship and how she loves her grandma. For many years, she has gone to sleep with the help of her grandmother's favorite songs and wakes to eat "Grandma's pancakes." Addison shares her grandmother's love of animals and talks about how her Grandmom would be proud of her abilities to care for her dog and cats. She even shares her grandmother's knack for telling a good story and knows how to creatively nurse the details to build a large and spell-binding epic.

Addison's connection to her grandmother has been typical of such relationships for many young children in that it provides her with a treasured legacy and a sense of community. What is different though about their connection is that Addison and her grandmother have never met in person. Addison's grandmother died in 1978, 15 years before her birth. Although Addison has not had the benefit of free baby-sitting services over the years, this has not stopped her from forming a strong connection with her grandmother.

Addison and I have stayed connected to her grandmother not just by keeping alive her stories through happenstance. Rather, we have actively sought others to participate in various aspects of story telling. Addison's memories and connections have been aided through the use of stories and songs that her great aunt has told her. She has sorted through pictures of her grandmother with her aunt and heard additional stories from her as well. Addison's Uncle has told her about her grandmother's jokes, puns, and musical interests. All have shared in the process of keeping grandmother alive for her.

New people enter our lives over time. As Addison took up membership in my (Lorraine's) life she was introduced to existing members in my club of life. These introductions were to both people who are living and to those who are no longer living. If we keep people's membership current, then introducing them over the years to new people who enter the circle only makes sense. We would not ignore an introduction to those who are living. Why would we ignore a person simply because they are dead?

REVISITING MEMORIES IN RESPONSE TO
DEVELOPMENTAL LIFE EVENTS

There may be times and events when a deceased person's membership goes by unnoticed. The rhythm of daily life fills our appointment books and leaves us with little room to notice, let alone create, ceremonies and rituals. Then there are other times when we strongly notice a person's membership in our lives. As our lives change, and take on new meanings and positions, we might find that these events call us to reinstate and renew a person's membership in our lives. For example, as a person graduates from college, they might grow increasingly aware of their deceased grandfather's voice of pride at accomplishing such a task. Or a young bride might report that she has elected to have their father's brother stand with her at her wedding as emissary for her deceased father.

As we think narratively about new events and changes, we can employ the strengths of story to navigate new terrain. We might call forward then the voice and wisdom that a deceased member can offer to us. Often, we carry with us in our heads the voice, words, and knowledge of deceased members. Without much effort at all, we can conjure up their advice in response to questions we might ask. We are able to access our "internalized other" voice and activate dialogue with them that continues to guide and comfort.

Before death, this person had their own "club of life." In these networks, there may be many who have access to particular stories and wisdom that can be beneficial. One woman explained that for years she did not much think of her deceased mother whose death had happened so long ago, when she was just a child. Then as she became pregnant with her first child, some 20 years after the death of her mother, she started "sensing her mother's presence." She became quite curious about what it must have been like for her mother to be pregnant 28 years ago with her. She also turned to her maternal Aunt to gain more information. She learned how her mother had welcomed her pregnancy and her daughter joyfully. Information that had not been previously brought to life was highlighted as it became important or needed. Her own pregnancy allowed her to renew the connection to her mother.

Here is another excerpt from the conversation with Justine that illustrates this point further.

> Justine: I think as I've got older and I've done things I've thought, well, how would Mum have done that? What would Mum have thought? Her voice is always there in the back of my mind.
>
> John: Is that a useful voice for you?
>
> Justine: Yes it is, lots of times. Cause it's got a good sense of humor and is very pragmatic. And sometimes I think, oh piss off. That's my business. I don't need that from you. She was a bit nosey at times. . . .
>
> John: So you've chosen certain parts of her that you want and other parts that you don't want.

Justine: Yeah, I have, yeah. And I think I particularly remember the humor and the stoicism.

John: What about for her? What do you now want to offer her?

Justine: I think I've kept her memory alive in lots of ways. Last night I got those photos out and I sat down with Tony and we talked about it and I remembered how much he remembered.

John: So you were working to keep her memory alive with him?

Justine: For the next generation, yeah. I gave my grandson photos of her.

John: So just imagine what it would be like for her to know that you were doing that with Tony last night. What would that be like?

Justine: Oh she would have loved it.

John: Really? What would it mean?

Justine: Well, it would have meant that I still remembered her. And she loved Tony. She had a real soft spot for him. He was only twelve when she died. He was going through his own trauma at that time. Being abused and all that. She didn't know about that and probably wouldn't have handled that at all well.

John: What would she say about how you've handled it?

Justine: Oh, she'd be astounded. She wouldn't expect that women could do things like that. But I don't think it's anything out of the ordinary, in some ways. I mean it's just what you do when one of your kids is hurt. And she would have felt the same way. She would have said, "Well, so? What do you expect to be doing?"

John: That was the ferociousness that she showed when you were hurt?

Justine: Yeah. So stop the hell worrying and get on with it. And I suppose I do that too. . . . So she's taught me about stickability in some ways too. She stuck with my father through some unbelievable stuff. But she still kept a sense of herself . . . until the later years. When Dad became intolerable to live with.

John: But she stuck with a sense of herself for a long time.

This conversation weaves back and forth between the present and the past, and even prefigures future remembering. It brings memories from long ago and updates them through collocation with current developments in conversations that are as recent as yesterday. What emerges is a plasticity of relationship with time.

Remembering then does not need to be a temporary phenomenon that fades after a brief while. It can continue on and take new life for years into the future. The dead can grow new relationships and develop existing ones through the medium of story. The key to this development lies in the extent to which remembering is built into conversation over time. In the next chapter, we shall focus on spiritual beliefs as a specific dimension of what can be included in such conversations.

CHAPTER EIGHT
Narratives of Spirituality

> A pilot stranded in the desert awakes one morning to see, standing
> before him, the most extraordinary little fellow. "Please," asks the
> stranger, "draw me a sheep." And the pilot realizes that when life's
> events are too difficult to understand, there is no choice but to
> succumb to their mysteries.
>
> (Antoine de Saint-Exupery, 1971, back cover)*

As we make sense of death, many of us call on one or more of the
versions of religious or spiritual transcendence that are available.
We take comfort and strength from convictions about life after
death, reincarnation, ancestral spirits, and the like. Others believe that
death brings personal existence to an end. These beliefs are matters
of both personal preference and cultural belonging. If we are in any
way interested in meaning construction as a significant aspect of the
experience of grief, these beliefs need to be taken into account. In
this chapter, we shall discuss how to include the spiritual narratives
that people hold dear in the process of constructing remembering
conversations.

Modernist psychology is rooted in a realist view of social science
and has often seemed to construct personhood with little regard for
people's spiritual commitments. Where these exist, they are frequently
assimilated into a realist framework as "cognitions," expressions
of "emotion," "superstitions," or even "religious delusions." A postmodern perspective invites us to see science itself as value-laden,
imbued with spiritual implications and inviting forward particular
allegiances, rather than as constructing truth in a separate domain
from religious or spiritual belief. One of the useful corollaries that flows

*Excerpt from *The Little Prince,* by Antoine de Saint-Exupery, copyright © 1943 by
Harcourt, Inc. and renewed 1971 by Consuelo de Saint-Exupery, English translation
copyright © 2000 by Richard Howard, reprinted by permission of Harcourt, Inc.

from this postmodern shift is that other truth claims (including religious ones) become more available than they were under the dominance of the scientific method.

However, it is recognized in the literature on death and bereavement that coming face to face with one's own death, or with the death of a loved one, often provokes experiences of transcendence from the straightforward world of the real and observable. By this, we mean that people are jolted into a sense of themselves as part of something larger than they had previously conceived (Richards, 2001). Carlos Castaneda, in *Journey to Ixtlan* (1972), squares off against the fear of death. His teacher, don Juan, somewhat quixotically, shows Castaneda how death shapes perspective and gives meaning to life.

> Death is the only wise adviser that we have. Whenever you feel, as you always do, that everything is going wrong and you're about to be annihilated, turn to your death and ask if that is so. Your death will tell you that you're wrong; that nothing really matters outside its touch. Your death will tell you, "I haven't touched you yet" (p. 55).

The hospice movement has encouraged people to explore and embrace spiritual meanings of death more than has conventional medical treatment (Richards, 2001). In hospices, spiritual beliefs and practices are included in conversations about people's experience of grief much more fully than they are recognized in the psychological literature.

Spiritual commitments do not always take the forms specified in organized religion either. People develop their spiritual identities through engagement with art, music, academic scholarship, business, and sport. They may experience strong connections with animals and nature. They feel compassion for the suffering of others and they express hope for a better world through acts of benevolence and altruism in a variety of forms. The fluidity of story makes it possible to honor and include a range of such spiritual meanings.

There are theological perspectives emerging too which place a significant emphasis on the place of narrative and discourse at the heart of religious or spiritual sensibility (for example, Cupitt, 2000; Geering, 1994). In one expression of this perspective, Lloyd Geering (1994) argues:

> Through language, story and the creation of a world, human consciousness has come to pursue its own quest for unified, meaningful and purposive existence. . . . If we choose to speak of God we shall be using this term to focus on all that we supremely value and on the goals which make human existence meaningful and worthwhile . . . (pp. 234-235).

We are sympathetic to this perspective and can see much value in its practical expression in the arena of remembering conversations. If professional conversations with the dying and the bereaved are going to grapple respectfully with what is meaningful and purposive for people, then they need to incorporate the religious metaphors and stories by which people organize their understandings of ultimate meaning.

In conversations that are informed by narrative and social constructionist practice, death can therefore be discussed within a context that includes and makes use of people's spiritual commitments. We can be less constrained by an empirical focus on the observable "here and now," or on what can be scientifically proven. We can be more curious about the complex realm of meaning-making that human beings inhabit. In this realm, there are many possible ways to account for the meaning of death. We assume that whatever spiritual or religious stories make sense to the people involved will have material effects in the relationships with others in their membership club. We think it is useful, therefore, to open up conversations about people's narrative accounts of life, death, and what occurs after we stop breathing (or whenever we define the moment when death occurs).

ADVANTAGES OF A NARRATIVE PERSPECTIVE

We do not need to prove the existence of an afterlife to know that, at the very least, people live on in story after death. In addition to whatever spiritual beliefs a person might endorse, the idea of an ongoing story can be a gateway to continuation of membership and lasting legacy. Story offers transcendence, regardless of religious persuasion. Those who live on carry the beliefs, the dreams, the hopes, and the love that were shared with the deceased, and these connections can be handed down from generation to generation. When people hold dearly to beliefs in some form of afterlife, these beliefs can be included as contextual features of these ongoing narratives.

We therefore advocate that remembering conversations and practices include a focus on a person's belief in what happens after life. How people construct an ongoing relationship with those who have died will in part hinge upon where they believe the dead to be. As practitioners, we need to inquire about a person's beliefs about an afterlife prior to that person's death, and also to inquire about family members' beliefs after death occurs. Such inquiry can invite the construction of meaning around spiritual beliefs in ways that people find comforting and sustaining.

Those who are about to die can answer such questions in a way that instructs friends and family where they can be found after death; as if leaving a kind of spiritual forwarding address. Such information can be made use of in the construction of remembering conversations. For example, if a person believes that, after death, they are heaven-bound, we might want to develop the implications of this belief in a narrative plot trajectory. We might ask whether they believe they will still be able to see their loved ones here on earth. We want to know whether the living can communicate with the deceased, or whether the deceased becomes a protective angelic force that is omnipresent. All of this information can become a source of rich description of the ongoing relational context for the person who is dying. It affirms the ongoing- ness of life. For the living, answers to questions like these can provide an important key to the relational map.

If we express curiosity about people's concepts of heaven, we can help them develop vague ideas into a narrative account and, in the process, maintain pathways of connection between the living and the deceased. Often, people think of heaven as a place from which a loved one can see them and hear them, but they may also need to know if they can talk with the living or send messages to them. People have surprisingly varied beliefs about such matters. It is worth developing a curiosity about them. The different possible meanings can each produce entire conversations about how we want to include a loved one in the ongoing communications of daily life, and in remembering rituals.

STORY TRANSCENDS RELIGIOUS CREED

For a person who has a strong religious practice, culturally available beliefs about death and afterlife will have been discussed many times throughout their life. However, a religious affiliation does not necessarily indicate a personal belief system. People often hold to particular beliefs in their own ways. It is possible, for example, to find those with a strong Christian or Jewish faith who have a secret place of belief in ideas like reincarnation. From a constructionist perspective, we are more interested in the meaning-making potential of the belief for the person than in the doctrinal correctness within the religious tradition. It is, therefore, important that we speak about these things, when possible, as they can serve as gateways to very important avenues in the process of making sense of death. As we open these important conversations, we can thicken the possible connections between friends and family members and increase the range of possibilities for the time after death. The following story illustrates this point.

BARBARA AND MATILDA

Barbara was 71 when she realized that she was going to die from the metastasized cancer she had had for over a decade. She was the only child of Matilda who was 95 and in very good health. Matilda's husband had died eight years previously and Matilda had moved in with her daughter at that time. This move helped both of them, as Matilda could no longer drive, and occasionally Barbara needed help around the house when her illness robbed her of energy.

They told me (Lorraine) they had been very close all their lives. Barbara expressed concern about how her upcoming death was going to be for her mother. She thought it would be emotionally hard and added that they were not talking about this eventuality. Barbara had had a few good days, because of a new medication she had started. But, she was worried that her mother might think she was getting better, rather than dying. She knew, however, that this energy was temporary and that the cancer would take her life soon. For Barbara, it was important that she trust God's will in this process. She said that her mother also knew this, and also trusted that what was to come would be for the best, because God had determined it.

Barbara had been raised by her mother, who was single at the time. Religion was important to them and they were active in a Southern Baptist community in Georgia. Matilda shared that it had, indeed, been hard on her to see her vibrant daughter taken away by illness. She added that she did not question God's will but that she was also praying to God every day that he would take her first, before her daughter.

I asked, "And what if, for some reason, that doesn't happen? What if God has a different intention?"

"I know this is a possibility but I don't know how I will handle that," said Matilda. "At one level, it will be OK, because I know that it is God's will. I can trust my faith in God. But on the other hand, I have always been very close with my daughter and I don't know what that will be like."

Matilda was tearful as she told me of this. Then she paused and asked me, "Do you have kids?"

I told her that I, like her, had one daughter also and that I could understand that sort of closeness. "What do you remember about your daughter when she was young," I asked.

She told me how Barbara was born in a rural part of Georgia at home. She spoke proudly of how she had breast-fed her baby, even though that had been discouraged then. She said her family and the midwife had tried to talk her out of it, but she had insisted. Then she said, "Do you know what it means to take a baby out?"

"No. What does that mean?"

Matilda shared with me that in African-American families, in the south of the Uunited States at the time that Barbara was born, a baby was supposed to remain hidden in the house where she was born, until someone introduced her to the world. This person who was selected to "take the baby out" became like a godparent and the baby was said to take on attributes of this person. Because of these important implications, Matilda had thought long and hard about who would do this for her infant daughter. When Barbara was one month old, Matilda had asked her only sister to take her baby out.

"Why did you choose your sister?" I asked.

Matilda replied that her sister was very kind, intensely religious, and very compassionate. She had wanted Barbara to take on these qualities in her life. She also wanted her sister to be strongly involved with her daughter.

"So how has Barbara taken on her qualities?"

She said that Barbara had many similarities to her sister. In fact, not only had her sister and her daughter held many things in common, but her sister had also died from cancer many years earlier. Matilda then returned to describing the taking-out ceremony. First, her sister took the baby to all parts of the house and then outside to each corner of the house. At each point, she stopped and asked God to look after Barbara throughout her life. As she carefully moved further from Barbara's house, she paused at points along the way to town to ask for blessings from God. She had blessed her in this way before she took her into town. There, the baby was introduced to members of their community and they, too, were asked for blessings to help Barbara in her life.

I asked Matilda if she thought her sister would be one of the persons waiting to greet Barbara on the other side after she died. "Do you think that your sister would be willing to take your daughter out again and to introduce her into this new world?"

Matilda was clearly touched by this idea. She thought that this would be helpful for Barbara to have a person that she could rely on in heaven. Although there were others they knew in heaven, Matilda thought it would be only right for her sister to take on this important task, as she had done so before.

I was curious about the implications of this thought. "If Barbara precedes you in death might she be willing to take *you* out into the new world, when the time comes for you to die?"

We talked for some time about this idea. Both mother and daughter had tears in their eyes as they spoke about how much this made sense to them. Barbara spoke about her closeness with her mother and how they were like sisters in some ways. In fact, she said, since they were both children of God, they were also sisters. Barbara liked the idea of being able to "bring her mother out" when the time came.

Matilda too sat well with this thought. "I wonder if that is what Princess Diana did for Mother Teresa. Before, when Mother Teresa died immediately following Princess Diana, I had thought Mother Teresa had gone to help Diana. But now I am thinking it might have been the other way around."

NEW MEANINGS

For Matilda, to think in this way brought relief from some anguish she was experiencing. She was able to form new meanings of her daughter's impending death. Its meaning was no longer contained within an idea of wrongful ordering, before her own death. The story of taking a baby out opened for her a new meaning that connected their afterlife with their history. It also afforded a different prospect of future in the hope that her daughter's death was not wasted and did not need to be thought of as wrongly ordered. There was room in her new construction for some anticipation of a post-mortem family reunion. Her comments about Princess Diana and Mother Teresa also suggested that the re-ordering she was doing stretched beyond her personal circumstances and included a shift in her cosmological understanding.

These new stories opened up, in part, because I had been curious and interested in the spiritual narratives that held meaning for these two people, even though these narratives were outside my own cultural frames of reference. Through these narratives, we were also able to explore a sense of ongoing location for their relationship. If Matilda wanted to "find" her daughter following death, she would know where to look to do so. She would be able to maintain relationship with her daughter, all the while being reassured that her sister was offering a protective wing for Barbara to rest under in heaven.

Matilda and I met two weeks later. I asked her if she was still asking God to take her first.

"Yes," she said. "I still want a miracle to happen. But now, I think I realize that my daughter will have a miracle. I just don't know if she is going to be here or in heaven when that happens."

WHAT DOES THIS MEAN FOR A PERSON WHO IS NOT RELIGIOUS?

In the way we construct narratives, there is no pre-requisite to believe in an afterlife. People do not have to make a decision about these complex issues in order to succeed in having a positive or meaningful death experience. Afterlife is guaranteed through the participation in stories and in renewed membership. How we continue to live on in narrative is one place where spirit can live.

For a person who may not believe in God or in an afterlife, the opportunity to continue forward in story can be a comfort. One gentleman prior to his illness, would have said that there was no God or afterlife. As he got close to death, his comment was that he was "leaving the door open to all possibility." For some, however, there is not an open door for this type of conversation. How do we address their needs of membership following death? Where can their loved ones find them following death?

EVAN

Evan knew in his heart that there was no God. In spite of his 12 years of active involvement with drug and alcohol treatment programs that emphasized the importance of "a higher power," he described himself as "an atheist." He said that all he knew was the present. After his diagnosis with liver cancer, he was concerned about what his spiritual choices meant. He was particularly concerned about his daughter who, as a young adult, was also involved in drugs and alcohol. He did not want her to follow in the footsteps that he felt were now costing him his life. He grappled with the perplexity of an afterlife as we spoke but would repeatedly return to stating that "this is all there is."

Over a few conversations, I (Lorraine) asked what it would mean to him if his daughter grew to know his story. How might she come to know Evan's story of spiritual struggle with drugs and alcohol? In particular, I wanted to know how his daughter might come to know about the hardships with which Evan had paid for his involvement with drugs. What price did he think he had paid besides liver cancer? We explored many areas and, at his request, I took notes that would be provided to Evan's daughter.

We also spoke about what it meant for Evan to choose the sobriety he had maintained for so many years. I asked what might his daughter have to rely upon if she too wanted to not choose drugs and alcohol? Together, we constructed an intricate story of the price Evan paid for his choices, as well as the strength and courage he needed to not live under the influence. As we did so, Evan grew more and more confident that his daughter would be all right. We plotted together who else might be available to remind his daughter in the future of the gains and losses of a drug and alcohol lifestyle.

THE LEGACY OF STORY

Evan's story became his legacy. It no longer mattered to Evan whether there was an afterlife as such. He felt content in knowing that his afterlife would come in the form of saving his daughter from the hardships he had known. Evan wanted to keep his voice alive for her—not in some glorified version of his years of excessive living, but as a mirror that he hoped she would use in making a new path. We used Evan's belief that the "here and now" mattered more than anything promised in an afterlife. It was from this spiritual place that we constructed his messages to his daughter. He constructed stories of hope from painful life experience for his daughter to keep her father's voice close to her.

When we think narratively, we are free to sit with many differing religious beliefs. As we construct with the dying or the bereaved places of ongoing membership that will matter in their club of life, we can include in these clubs a variety of religious and spiritual practices and beliefs. The practices simply act as guideposts to point the way on the road of remembering. We can utilize these beliefs as sources of comfort that enhance membership and render it transcendent. A person may be practicing Christianity or not, or practicing Buddhism and believing in re-incarnation, or may believe that they will continue to live on through the garden and plants that their ashes might fertilize. All of these beliefs have equally valid narrative utility and can provide us with places to join in the construction of remembering conversations.

WHEN A FAMILY HAS MORE THAN ONE RELIGIOUS PERSPECTIVE

Not uncommonly, a family, or a club of membership, may include a range of differing spiritual and religious perspectives. Often, these differences are not problematic in the course of daily life and people manage to live side by side without conflict. However, such differences can have dramatic implications for how people relate to each other as death approaches. Sometimes, different spiritual beliefs create contradictory afterlife locations and meanings. The following story illustrates this point.

MIKAILA

Mikaila was raised in the Jewish faith in Eastern Europe. She had left there, as a young woman, to find opportunities in America. When she was 24, she met and fell in love with Frank. They married and spent a full life together, raising their three children. Now, distant from the community that supported her Judaism, Mikaila grew more interested in practicing at Frank's Christian church and was baptized as a Protestant. Yet, it was not until her diagnosis with terminal cancer that she and Frank spoke about their beliefs in an afterlife. I (Lorraine) sat with them and invited them to address this hitherto unspoken topic.

"Mikaila, where is it that you imagine you will be following your physical death?" I asked.

"Nowhere. I think this is it and I will not be anywhere after this."

Frank was shaken by her answer. "What do you mean? I thought we were going to be in heaven together."

When I asked Frank to explain, he told me their shared history. "I thought that you and I were going to meet again. That is what I have told the children and what I assumed to believe. I guess I am surprised, too, because I thought that we shared the same beliefs through the church."

Mikaila explained that she knew that Frank thought they were going to heaven, but that this belief did not quite fit for her. She was more comfortable thinking about her Jewish beliefs as a young girl. From that perspective, she was more interested in valuing her relationship presently, rather than thinking about something yet to come after she died.

"If you are not going to be in Heaven, then where will I find you?" Frank asked.

Mikaila's answer was loving and opened possibility for continued connection. "I will be all around you—in our home and in our children and our grandchildren. And I hope I will be in your heart for the rest of your life too."

I met with Frank two weeks after Mikaila's death. I was very curious about what had come from our previous conversations. What new meanings and connections had grown as a result of our talks?

Frank shared with me that just prior to Mikaila's death, he was certain that Jesus visited her. He said he could tell by the peaceful feeling that was with the two of them as she died. In these moments, he felt that he had a kind of awakening as well. With the realization that Mikaila had been the beneficiary of "the love of Jesus," he saw that it did not matter whether her "visitation" was Christian or Jewish. These new thoughts inspired him as they planned her memorial service. He carefully included prayers from both traditions—the Lord's prayer and the Jewish Kaddish for the dead—to embrace both traditions. He also invited Mikaila's family to their home to sit Shivah, the seven day period of Jewish prayers after a loved one's death.

Family members do not always have such beautiful answers, or blendings of divergent practices, when religious and spiritual differences are brought into focus in the face of death. However, it can be crucially important to the shape of ongoing relationship to negotiate such meanings. Professionals who meet people in these circumstances can assist by being curious about the detail of personal meanings. As these meanings are brought into conversation, even if there are differences in family beliefs, they can be incorporated into the relationship as we affirm ongoing membership in our clubs. When people are struggling with contentious and divisive perspectives, as professionals we need to take care to stay curious about the sometimes subtle points of connection they can establish in order to have continued access to ongoing relationship.

Spiritual beliefs can help families look toward ongoing relationship. They can point the way to connection before and after death. As the following account tells, however, spiritual beliefs can also be important in context of an individual facing his own death. We can utilize his narratives to bring further meaning and comfort in the transition that death brings.

SAMUEL

Samuel was in his late forties. He had been ill for many years with numerous chronic ailments, including heart problems, diabetes, and cancer. When we met, he lived in a small trailer with his uncle, who had agreed to care for him. Samuel had no other family, as they, too, had all died young. Because of Samuel's many illnesses, he had led a life that was often isolated from other people. He had not worked in over 20 years and had never dated. He explained that he enjoyed reading the Bible and found peace in this activity. When he first became ill, at about 20 years old, he said he had become "born again" through accepting

Jesus as his savior. This was very important for Samuel, as it gave him a place of hope. He felt that Heaven would be his answer to a life that had been challenging at times.

As we spoke over the month or so prior to his death, he shared doubts that he might "not be a good enough Christian" to get into heaven. He was concerned about thoughts and activities that occurred long before he converted to Christianity. These thoughts gnawed at him and kept him awake at night. In fact he feared that God might judge him harshly and he could end up in hell.

These thoughts were very troubling for Samuel. The meaning that he had made about his future needed some peace for the quality of his life to be restored. A revision was needed. When we spoke about this, Samuel described how he understood God to be. He thought of God as very loving and smart. I asked him if God would be able to forgive him for any possible wrongdoings that he thought he had committed. He, of course, said that God would.

I asked him an internalized other question to invoke the voice of God in him, "How do you think God might explain your earlier choices?"

Samuel was able to talk about his choices in his youth as not being influenced by his studies from the Bible. The voice of God spoke about Samuel as a new man and said that there was room for his change of heart and change of actions after he was baptized.

I asked him, "If this is so, then do you expect that God will allow you into heaven?"

Samuel said that, in fact, he knew God would have him in heaven.

We decided, then, that perhaps we needed to keep God's voice closer to Samuel during his dying and to include God's vote as way of membering God for Samuel. It gave him a great deal of comfort to think about God as being more forgiving then he could allow himself to be. When he would wake at night with worries, this is what Samuel would remind himself of.

METAPHORS OF MEANING

It was not necessary for me to hold the same beliefs as Samuel in order to inquire into the meanings that might be of comforting significance for him. However, I did need to enter his world of meaning and to utilize the metaphors in which it was constructed. Developing a narrative account of the afterlife, as it existed in his personal meaning system, played a part in the construction of the quality of his life in the days and weeks before his death.

This story also illustrates how the voices that have significance in the club of our lives need not always be those of living human beings. In Samuel's case, the voice of God had been strongly incorporated into his club of life, as a result of his Bible studies. Others may have voices of influential ancestors, prophetic teachers, the Virgin Mary, saints, favorite poets, or multiple gods that they can call on as resources in their struggles to make sense of death.

Remembering conversations are not always, however, being constructed in contexts where love and goodwill abound. Life is more complex than that. In the next chapter, we shall examine some aspects of life that can make for more troubling memories and suggest some ideas for focusing remembering in these contexts.

CHAPTER NINE

Troubling Memories

> Tomorrow, his first poems in book form will be with you—the immortality of his great soul. What a wonderful moment it will be for you, though an agony too.
>
> *Edith Sitwell to Mrs. Owen on the anniversary of the*
> *death of her son, Wilfred Owen, 3 November 1919*
> (Harding & Dyson, 1981, p. 146)*

Our relationships are not always full of good memories. Even the best of relationships have times of discomfort or difficulty. All of us, too, have seen, or experienced, relationships that are worse than simply uncomfortable. Occasionally relationships may be riddled with displeasure or anger. Some relationships have dimensions that are harmful and destructive. As we have addressed issues of membership, we have often appeared to assume that the connection with the deceased was a positive one—or, at least, one where there were some positive aspects that they might wish to carry forward in memory. This is clearly not always the case.

In this chapter, we shall address some common relational contexts that people find problematic in remembering conversations. When we teach, we are regularly questioned about these aspects. People often feel uneasy about positive acts of remembering those with whom their relationships have been abusive, for example. How is it that the concept of membership and the practice of remembering can benefit these deaths and relationships as well? We shall address this question by including some of the more common questions we receive in workshops and classes. The questions come from counselors, ministers,

---

*From *A Book of Condolences: Classic Letters of Bereavement,* edited by Rachel Harding and Mary Dyson, © 1981 by the editors. Reprinted by permission of The Continuum Publishing Group.

physicians, social workers, psychologists, nurses, and students from around the world.

1. How does this way of thinking work when the relationship was a particularly difficult one?

It is sometimes hard to make sense of relationships that are tumultuous. Staying connected to a relationship that was fraught with conflict and pain is not always our first inclination. If a connection has been painful and tricky, if not downright undesirable, in life, how can we suggest handling such memories after death?

While relationships are not always consistently good, neither are they usually consistently bad. We would speculate that even challenging relationships can have, at times, redeeming qualities. We can see two possible ways to re-evaluate the membership status of someone that we have found difficult.

First, we might be interested in exploring the multi-dimensionality of the connection. Significant relationships can be expected to have a series of contexts and events about which stories can be told. It might be beneficial to think of the relationship as existing in many different forms and that any one story about the relationship is likely to be only partial. Any particular story must leave out some aspects of experience and there is always unstoried experience that can be called upon (Bruner, 1986). If we explore the range of possible stories that can be told, we can become interested in the different effects that the varying versions have for those involved in the remembering. It can be worth noticing what happens to the problematic story when we take note of other stories. We do not want to do this at the expense or exclusion of a significantly difficult or abusive story, but we do want to pry open a space for new stories to emerge as well. It is possible to make decisions about which stories to privilege. We can construct conversations that deliberately include stories that, in years to come, might grow into new themes that sit alongside the theme of difficulty. Neither the difficult story nor the more positive one need to be settled on as the true story. They can simply exist side-by-side in memory for us to remember as we choose, or as they serve particular purposes in our lives.

For example, Shakira explained the week before her mother died, "My mother never understood me. She said I was 'strange.' Long ago, I gave up feeling like my mother would approve of me—or looking to her for approval. She was a housewife. She did not need to work, because her husband supported her. As a single mother, I had to work. I also like my work as an artist. She doesn't understand my painter's lifestyle and that I keep odd hours, for example. She doesn't understand my drawings, or what I need to do to make one. It is something that is foreign for her."

I (Lorraine) wondered about places where their story had other prospects as well, "Where do the two of you fit? Are there places where you can see eye to eye?"

Shakira thought about this, "Sometimes, we can talk about current events, politics, and music. It is not often, but once in a while we can have a nice conversation. I recall a time a couple of years ago when she came to one of my art shows. I was shocked that she was there. I never asked her about this—about why she came. Now she is dying. I don't talk to her about that either. I just sit with her and hold her hand."

"If you could talk with her about her decision to come to your art show, what do you think she might say about this?"

"You know, I think she would say she was curious. She would say that she wanted to know what I did in the evening. She wanted to know what her daughter did with her life."

"And, what do you suppose she found there? I mean, was she surprised by what she saw with your art?"

"I have no doubt," Shakira laughed. "My mother didn't know that some of my art included nudes. I think she liked it but was a little shocked too."

This was a clear example of a plot event that did not fit with Shakira's dominant story of relationship with her mother. Because it did not fit, it was hard for this aspect of their relationship to grow and be incorporated without a spotlight being shone upon it. White and Epston (1990) would call this a unique outcome, or an exception to a dominant story. To emerge from obscurity, it needed to be built into a conversation. Had we simply dismissed the connection between Shakira and her mother as being a poor fit, or dysfunctional, or abusive, Shakira might have missed future opportunities. By asking questions that looked for stories other than the dominant "bad fit" story, we got to know particular places where she might come to appreciate her mother. It freed her to know her mother through different lenses and gave her a richer range of stories through which to pursue this relationship. These stories can even establish a new kind of membership for her mother. We might even hold out places of hope that this relationship will become closer, long after her mother dies, as Shakira continues to remember and incorporate new knowledge about her mother.

There is another path that may be considered as we remember difficult relationships. There may be times when it does not serve a person to remember in ways that reinstate the deceased person, or restore privileged membered status. To do so could create further harm for the person who is alive. In these circumstances, it may be of benefit to keep the deceased person's membership further away and to build remembering around that more distant, less intimate membership position. Membership may continue to be granted to a deceased person, but membered status may need to take on peripheral or provisional features.

In those instances, the focus can be shifted to how the living person navigated such a challenging relationship. We still would be interested in inquiring, from a strength-based perspective, into what learnings or possible benefits came from the connection. We might want to know, for example, how a person has used adverse relationship experiences to make distinctions that helped form other more satisfying connections. The focus might be directed at the resources the person gained and how these translate into daily choices and actions. How is it that they are stronger, smarter, and make better life choices as a result of a difficult relationship? We do not want to trivialize the effects of challenging relationships or abusive circumstances. However, we do want to foreground the resilience and courage that people develop, even in the midst of the harshest of life circumstances.

In this way, we are still redefining membership. We ask questions about a larger audience who understood what it took to take this action.

We might ask, "Who noticed the steps you took?"

"Was there anyone in particular who helped prepare you to take these steps?"

"What might they say about the strength/courage that you needed to take this action?"

"Who else might know that you were capable of creating such an action in your life?"

"What has it meant to you to have these people cheering you on?"

The focus of such remembering is not on the relationship itself that created the hardship, but on the positive effects that accrue from reflections and learnings that flow from it. There have been many others who have written about these aspects of relational inquiry when there has been an abusive or destructive aspect to the connection. We do not wish to recapitulate all of these ideas, but to acknowledge that membership still must be accounted for when death arrives. We still are asked to make sense of relationship and place connections in a context that is beneficial.

Recently I (Lorraine) worked briefly with a family whose father was dying. He had been very distant for years from two of his four children. His wife explained there had been a messy divorce and years of limited contact with the two children. She said that one of the other two children did call them from time to time with updated information and then, subsequently, to let them know when this man died. They never elected, though, to visit or make contact with him prior to death. We (the wife and two children) speculated that the estranged children felt too hurt and angry over wounds from 20-some years previously.

Had I had the opportunity to interview these adult children, I would have most likely been curious about the circumstances that led to their distance. I perhaps would have discussed with them the other stories that their siblings knew about their father. Had I found out, as I suspected from the conversations we did have, that this man was at times very difficult to live with, I would have asked additional questions, similar to those listed above that establish audienceship in larger circles. Such questions glean and bring forward the best possible stories of strength, resilience, hope, and courage.

2. What if the person who died was physically, sexually, or emotionally abusive?

Membership granted by biological birthright does not guarantee an automatic lifelong privileged status. We often assume that we are entitled to access in another person's life because we are related. If that were the case, membership would be determined solely through biology and could not be revoked. There certainly are those who might make this claim, but we prefer not to agree. We think of membership as more flexible. It is constructed through social processes and is best thought of as a privilege. Anthropology has taught us that there are many possible cultural patterns of relatedness and that biological connections are only given meaning within cultural practices. Rather than being a static given, membership may be earned and learned through significant interactions at many different points throughout life. It is not uncommon for membered status to be altered or even revoked if infractions of membership rules occur.

Change in membership status might be instigated when persons grow less close over the years. Sometimes there can be a change in status following a relationship break-up or divorce, when relations with former partners and in-laws are revised. There may be a change in membership status originating from an abuse of power where the membered status has been used to exploit, tyrannize, or hurt another. When these things occur, as they do with relationships that include sexual, physical, and emotional abuse, the privilege of membership is called into question. If there is no other way for the relationship to exist (other than as an expression of power where one or more persons are denied a legitimate voice), it can be beneficial to distance a person's membership. Even if someone's membership cannot be revoked completely, it can be moved closer to the periphery of one's life, where it does not carry the same rights of intimacy that it once did. This process may have begun while a person is alive and physical death provides the opportunity to re-visit the degree of desired distance. Perhaps, death removes the possibility of any new abuses and puts the relationship on a different footing. Even so, a review of suspended membership rights and responsibilities at the time of death may still be warranted.

3. **What about people who have illnesses that impact on or interfere with memory, such as Alzheimer's? Can we use remembering practices for people who have been unable to connect with their memories prior to their physical death?**

For loved ones of a person who has had memory problems, their "death" often seems to come long before their physical demise. As deterioration of mental faculties occurs, people may cease to recognize their family or be responsive to them in familiar and loving ways. These situations are a perfect opportunity to incorporate remembering practices. If we assume that remembering is not an individual psychological process but one that happens in relationship, then we can take up the task of remembering on behalf of someone who is struggling to do so, just as we help push others in wheelchairs when they cannot be completely in charge of their own locomotion. Remembering conversations can serve the function of reincorporating a person's thoughts, feelings, stories, and presence into their communities, even when they are struggling to achieve this on their own behalf. In this way, we all benefit from these actions prior to death as well.

We can also use this idea of relational remembering for people whose illness has taken over their bodies but left their mental faculties intact. Illnesses like A.L.S., multiple sclerosis, strokes, and Parkinson's disease often leave a person cut off from their ability to control their limbs and from the ability to speak or write. As there are many people who make up membership communities, others can bring to life stories, memories, and events for a person who can no longer communicate. Relationships can be enhanced by the deliberate telling of stories in the hearing of persons who are dying and unable to speak themselves.

One family gathered friends, relatives, and children together for a fiftieth wedding anniversary. The husband had been unable to speak or write for two years as a result of severe Parkinson's disease which had left him almost paralyzed. His wife was able to occasionally tell what he wanted and they were able to communicate in a telepathic fashion and through small facial gestures. This process was particularly excruciating for them, because he had been very gregarious in life and had made his living in sales. His wife shared how he had loved to tell stories and be around people. For the years he could not speak, she felt as though he had grown depressed.

When his family planned their anniversary party, they invited close friends and relatives, many of whom had been at their wedding. His wife requested that the guests arrive with stories ready. Throughout the evening, each person took a turn to tell what it meant to know them as a couple and to retell the husband's jokes and accomplishments. Even though he could not speak, others brought his "voice" to life and recounted numerous versions of the couple's life together. His membership in everyone's life was storied and his participation in the remembering was in the role of listener.

4. What about babies who die at birth, or shortly after, or through miscarriages? What about abortions? How might we use remembering practices for them?

The realist assumption would insist that we cannot have a remembering conversation with someone who died as a baby prior to being able to speak. From a constructionist perspective, this circumstance may make the task more arduous, but not impossible. Remembering is much more than the recapitulation of words that the deceased may have spoken. It is more like a process of breathing life into the meaning of a person's existence. For a baby who did not have the chance to articulate in words the meaning of her own life, the meaning can exist in the hopes and visions that her parents and her significant community held for her.

Remembering these hopes and visions can be an active process that solidifies the relationship with the child through affirmation and love. When a baby is born, he is already a member of a community through the many conversations that have already taken place around him. If he dies at birth or is miscarried, his membership still exists in the community which has talked about him. Excited parents may have told others of their upcoming birth, made important life decisions around the birth, or constructed private hopes about what the child will mean to them. Membership can even be granted long before conception through the articulation of hopes and dreams of a family. These hopes and dreams can be remembered and kept alive, even when a child dies.

In an Australian workshop, a woman shared how she had not spoken of her son for 27 years after he died at birth. She said, though, that there was not a day that went by that she did not think of him or wish him well. She felt grateful that she had been his mother, even if for only a short while, as his membership in her life highlighted her unquestionable love for children. She had learned from this that she wanted to be a teacher and carried this knowledge of her son's significance with her in her classroom with young children. Her son's membership was very much alive in all she did!

I (John) had a daughter, Julia, who died at four months old. At first, I was captured by meanings of loss around her death. It hurt greatly to contemplate the many opportunities that her death had taken away. I would never get to see her grow, read her stories, teach her to walk and talk, see her school reports, or watch her play with friends, let alone grow to adulthood and establish for herself a career and a family of her own. The sadness of this loss was almost unbearable at first.

Over the years, I have come to remember her differently than through the lens of this sadness. Sure, these losses still exist. But I also know that I have had many experiences in life as a result of her death that I treasure greatly. Julia has had a lot to say to me about my relationships with my other children. There are many people I have met as a result of her part in my life, some of whom have also had a child who died. Conversations about this experience have cemented some significant connections that I value greatly. I like to think that in this way Julia has introduced me to many people I would not otherwise have formed these connections with. In this sense, she has played a rich part in the development of my identity. Her meaning to me continues to grow as a result. And my relationship with her continues to grow as well. It was not the life that I expected to remember when she was born. But the remembering of her has certainly enriched my life far more than a focus solely on what I lost when she died would allow.

This is not to say that it was not tremendously unsettling to experience the death of a young child and the process of meaning reconstruction (Neimeyer, 2001) did not happen overnight. Jane Waldegrave (1999) also speaks of the challenge to the expected story of family life that a child's death brings. She coined the term "settled stories" to describe the meaning reconstruction that she achieved through her search for a change in meaning following the death of her five-year-old son, Jack.

> With Jack's death, my thinking changed, and has had an impact on my practice. I have tried to develop a workable alternative to traditional grief models. I have termed this alternative as working towards "settled stories." . . . I had to weave something for myself that fitted with my "knowing" and my need for connection, that

had meaning for me. When I did, something started to settle within myself (Waldegrave, 1999, p. 177).

5. Is it useful to acknowledge death anniversaries?

As words can carry meaning and significance, so too can dates. The meanings we collect around specific dates provide opportunities to bring a person's membership closer. Dates like birthdays, wedding anniversaries, and death dates can act as catalysts to the performance of rituals and ceremonies—both public and private—that are honoring of the person who has died and their place in the community.

The anniversary death date can be used as a benchmark for behavior. Ideas about when a person can be complete with their grief and officially move forward, for example, get wedded to these dates. Prescriptive formulas are developed about when a person can move, give away items that belonged to the deceased, remove a wedding band, or remarry. All get trapped within the implications of an anniversary date. We would suggest that the assumptions in each of these areas be deconstructed. As a guideline, we suggest that anniversaries be acknowledged in order to revisit the relationship with the deceased and to reclaim membership.

6. I felt relieved following the death of my father. Is this all right and can I use remembering conversations in that circumstance?

Feeling relief when someone dies is not an uncommon experience after the death of a loved one, particularly when the death has been from a difficult illness or has been painful. Families may be relieved that their loved one is no longer suffering. Or they may feel relief about not having to do the difficult work of caring for an ill family member. Or relief may relate to the suspense involved in a long drawn-out death story. The story of relief may be understandable for many other reasons too.

People sometimes get concerned that relief is part of their experience. They fear being judged for an improper or cold-hearted response. Relief is often not legitimated in professional discourse and lay literature as a normal response. Therefore, people can be caught off-guard when they or other family members feel this way and can have guilt invited forward. Others are unsure of how to respond when a family member honestly expresses this sentiment. It may contrast with a story of long-suffering that is fixed in everyone's minds. Therefore, the experience of "relief" may not be accorded the status of an acceptable response to death. Professionals can help by validating relief and legitimizing it through their acknowledgment.

A constructionist perspective does not require us to understand emotions like relief as essential truths about a person or a relationship, but as elements of one possible story. From a constructionist perspective, our feelings are produced within discourse and out of stories. Therefore, the story of relief may be one story, but there may be others as well, which can produce different emotional responses. The strength of feeling does not need to indicate the degree of truth value that we should accord a story. Stories of relief, of sadness, and of joy can sit alongside each other without us having to decide which is true and without any requirement to integrate them. Constructionism does not place great importance on the possibility, let alone the desirability, of integration, preferring different stories to be free to compete with each other for a person's attention. Regardless of the immediate reaction to a loved one's death, incorporating that person's memory and stories remains relevant.

7. How does narrative therapy work for people dying from AIDS?

Remembering practices can be highly political when the person who is dying has an illness that is linked with processes of social marginalization. Often, families whose family member has died from AIDS are left without places to speak about their loved one's death. A normalizing societal gaze pertains even after their deaths and families may be left explaining the circumstances of the disease. People who die from AIDS are still sometimes judged as willing contributors to their own death. Families sometimes revoke their memberships and, after their deaths from AIDS, excommunicate them altogether. A gay man may have been estranged from his family by living an alternative lifestyle which distances his membership. His subsequent AIDS death may be blamed on a lifestyle not sanctioned in his family or community. Families who do want to remember their loved one are often left without places to do so, as the gaze of dismemberment can be starkly judgmental. Lack of a legitimate audience silences people's desire to speak about AIDS and about people who die from it.

Some AIDS awareness projects have attempted to stand up to the silencing effects of marginalization. The AIDS quilt has traveled around North America and been displayed at communities nationwide; 44,000 quilt panels, each representing one life, have been designed to remember people who have died from this disease. Displaying the quilt and celebrity fundraisers has been used to keep visible people who have died from AIDS. Statements such as these are examples of what Myerhoff (1978, 1986) called "definitional ceremonies"; that is, ritual events by which a community of people actively creates a public validation of identity for its members. The Dulwich Centre, in Adelaide, Australia, has also taken up the creation of definitional ceremonies through their efforts to re-language and re-tell the stories of people with AIDS "living positive lives" (Denborough & White, 2000).

8. How do these ideas apply to situations where the death was by suicide or murder?

We can remember a person after their death, regardless of the events that contribute to the physical demise. The principles are the same. The question to be asked is about how we want to stay connected to those who have died. Even in the midst of tragic circumstances, there may be benefits from growing this connection. As with AIDS, it is important to avoid dismembering people from their loved ones and communities by focusing only on the way in which they died.

The meanings attached to the cause of death are not inconsequential. One woman told me (Lorraine) how she was attending a grief group following the death of her husband. During the group's opening, all participants would introduce themselves, tell the name and relation of the person who died and the cause of death. Each week when she had to state "cocaine overdose," she was overwhelmed with tears.

She was aware of what others might be thinking. She wondered if they were secretly thinking she too was using drugs, or that she was complicit in her husband's death. These internal dialogues pained her deeply, but before we talked about it she was not aware of how this introduction was curtailing her description of her relationship with her husband. He had been dismembered from her as she was separated from memories of all the good they had shared and the kindness he had shown her and their children. In a remembering conversation, she deconstructed these limitations and began to introduce her husband in ways that more richly described their lives and their love.

When someone takes their own life, the temptation to make sense of their lives in terms like "failure" can be very strong. The tragedy narrative can start to take over to the extent that people start to interpret many other events in a person's life as leading up to taking their own life. Suicide becomes the denouement that all other plot events are lined up with. How a person dies can start to dominate the meaning of his or her life, and other stories can be backgrounded in the process. The result can be a narrowing of attention to the possibilities for remembering.

To reverse this narrowing requires the opening up of a much richer story of remembering. Rather than a dominating story of a life leading up to suicide that renders all other life stories incomprehensible, the suicide one might be restoried as an event which does not have to blot out all the other stories about that person's meaningful actions and relationships.

The suicide itself can still be hard to make sense of. Family members may need to piece together a story of how things came to this pass which enables them to maintain respect and understanding for their deceased loved one.

Professionals can make a big difference in this process. Michael White tells some stories of therapeutic conversations with family members who have lost a loved one to suicide. In one example, in which he records a remembering conversation with a family whose daughter had died at her own hand (White, 2001), a conversation develops around understanding the qualities that the family knew in their daughter that made her determination to take her life understandable and fitting with how she had approached life. Many of these qualities were, in other circumstances, ones that they could admire. In the process of building this story of admiration of these qualities, even though they had been implicated in her death, the death was rendered more understandable, especially in the light of some of the things she was struggling with. One outcome of the conversations that this family had with Michael White was the calling of a gathering of their extended family in which they talked with everyone about their daughter's death and "rendered it sensible" (p. 17) to everyone present.

Similarly, murder and violent death can leave loved ones grasping for connection in a stark situation. They are often left isolated and silenced by the horror and fear that can grip a community. Murder is a harsh word and people often want to shy away from it, often shying away from those affected by it as well. Monk, Neylon, and Sinclair (in press) have documented this experience for people whose loved one has been murdered, and they draw attention also to the story themes that may be particular to this form of death. Often media attention and legal processes change the context and, therefore, the meaning of the grief experience. Anger with the perpetrator of the murder may be felt or expressed as a desire for revenge, and this desire can engage with a variety of responses. Sometimes, family members of murder victims have experienced premature pressure to forgive the person who has done the murder when they express vengeful impulses. The murderer may also be a family member and, therefore, membership status may need to be revised in many ways. All of these contextual features can affect the shape of the experience of grief, in which case remembering conversations need to take different shape. But the principle remains the same. The nature of the death should not take precedence over the appreciation of the life of the loved one. In fact, for people whose loved one dies in violent circumstances, it is all the more important to create on-going membership opportunities. To do so can mean claiming the importance of the murdered person's life back from being defined only by the awful way in which he or she died.

9. What do we do when the biological family is no longer "the club" for the person who died?

Membership is often comprised of large networks of people, only some of whom might be biologically related. For most people, their club of life includes significant relationships with friends, co-workers and neighbors, and church communities. Their club may also include people they have never met, like authors or politicians they admire. And their club may include people who have been dead for some time, or spiritual influences, such as angels or God.

Our interest in membered status makes us curious to understand who will carry the stories for the person who is dying. Narrative legacies can be bequeathed and fostered in many communities besides biological communities.

10. What about the timing of asking questions about remembering? Is it possible to ask about the positive aspects too soon? Does it interfere with the processing of sadness?

The idea of asking questions that deliberately seek out resources and strengths is not intended to silence sadness. It is still important to offer compassionate witnessing (Weingarten, 2000) to people in times of sadness. As practitioners, we must learn how to acknowledge and comment on stories of both sadness and joy. However, our preference is that sadness not be the *only* emotion that is acknowledged. In many stories of death, this is the case. The effects of this are far too limiting for honoring ongoing membership. We can do people a disservice if we encourage them to linger, or even dwell, in the experience of sadness in the belief that this will lead to a "healing" of grief.

Even in the face of death, there are many stories immediately available to us, as well as the story of loss. For example, we might want to know how the person will tell the story of the moment when death arrived in years to come. We can inquire, from a perspective of sometime in the future looking back, about what gave a person strength and courage at this time. Invitations such as this do not eliminate sadness, but they do recontextualize it and redirect our emotional focus to include many hopeful opportunities for future meaning-making.

11. How can we counsel family and friends when only a few people attend the funeral of a loved one?

There are times when funerals are sparsely attended. Not all are large gatherings. As people age, they may simply outlive their family and friends. They may have relocated from where they grew up and few of their old friends are able to attend. The limited number of attendees need not reflect the caliber of a person's life.

We can remember a person in this instance by bringing to life all the various memberships that have held meaning for the deceased. The membership club can be populated through stories of accomplishments and connections. We would encourage ministers and funeral directors to use this time to grow remembering. They can find out about the person's membership club prior to the service, in order to bring forward these stories. Those who do attend can be invited to share stories of their personal connection with the deceased.

One minister told how he preached a sermon to an audience of one—the deceased's spouse. As he was planning the service, he interviewed her and learned of the strong love that grew in their 60-year marriage. Their only child had been killed many years before and they had outlived most of their friends. Like the minister's father, the deceased man had worked as a carpenter.

During the funeral, the minister read scripture and sang a hymn and then sat with this man's widow. He shared with her what it meant to him to be introduced to her husband. Even though they had only met after this man's death, he was certain that he learned a lot from this man. He recalled special times with his own father.

This minister offered a great gift to this woman. Even though there were no other living people available to attend the funeral, he made the occasion meaningful by affirming the dead man's membership for her and by offering to carry forward his membership in his own life.

There are many more questions that we have been asked. In this chapter, we have addressed just a few concerns that arise most frequently. This is far from an exhaustive list but we hope that this clarifies the value of remembering conversations even in problematic contexts.

CHAPTER TEN
The Beginning

"It won't be the same, I say, not being able to hear you talk.
"Ah talk . . ."
He closes his eyes and smiles.
"Tell you what. After I'm dead, you talk. And I'll listen."
(Mitch Albom, 1997, p. 170)

Given what we have been saying in this book, the final chapter will not be a place to say good-bye. As with other journeys in life, this one does not end here. If you have come this far with us, we imagine that you have engaged in your own conversation with the ideas that we have been showcasing. Our hope is that the dialogue in which we are participating right now, as writers and readers, will live on. Perhaps, it will live on in your professional work. Perhaps, we may meet some day and talk in person about your responses to what we have said. We are certainly conscious that many other voices have contributed to the membership club that we have drawn from in the writing of this book. Writing these words has often involved a remembering of the contributions that others have made to our own understandings.

This final chapter is also not about reaching for a tidy closure. There are many other things that we could write more about. There are more stories to tell and further explanations to make. Some of them are ours and some are yours. There does, however, need to be a time to leave off any particular utterance and let it do its work in the ongoing production of discourse. Before we do so, there are just a few speculative thoughts to add.

Our interest in remembering conversations lies in their invigorating quality. Even in the midst of the most poignant crises of death, we have witnessed people becoming their best through remembering in richly evocative ways those that populate their membership clubs. We do not believe, therefore, that remembering is a casual process that simply whiles away time. It is a site of cultural production. Through remembering, relationships are enhanced and developed, even if one party is no longer alive. It is also a community-building process through which cultural renewal can take place and political stands can be made.

We are also interested in what happens to identities after people die. Survivors can come to know their dead loved ones in new ways. In this sense, the known identity of this person changes. Bakhtin illustrates this point by saying that Shakespeare, the great writer, is different from the identity of Shakespeare, the writer in his own day. Bakhtin (1986) says:

> We can say that neither Shakespeare himself nor his contemporaries knew that "great Shakespeare" whom we know now. . . . He has grown because of that which actually has been and continues to be found in his works, but which neither he himself nor his contemporaries could consciously perceive and evaluate in the context of the culture of their own epoch (p. 4).

Through the centuries since Shakespeare's death, his life and work have grown and developed through being remembered. His life has entered a different kind of relationship with time than it had in his own lifetime. Bakhtin refers to this shift as entering "great time."

It is not hard to think of many other famous artists who are known differently in death than they were in their own lifetimes. Think of Beethoven's shiftless life or of van Gogh's intense struggles with relationship and love. Or think of Rembrandt dying penniless in a world that had not yet developed an identity clothed in greatness for him. All of these people have since entered Bakhtin's "great time" and are now remembered in this light. The dross of their lives has dropped away and receded in significance. Their story has continued to take on fullness after death.

What is it that enables this process to happen in "great time," as Bakhtin calls it? We would speculate about "greatness" as a product of conversation, or of many conversations. There is something about the nature of dialogue that enhances any work. As Bakhtin again suggests, the fullness of a person's consciousness awakens, only when "wrapped in another's consciousness" (Bakhtin, 1986, p. 138). In the process of conversation, remembering takes place and the artist, through her work, becomes membered in the lives of many people, even across cultural barriers. Through the telling of many stories, a consensus gets distilled and refined. In the midst of the many details of life in the present, this distilling is somehow harder to achieve.

We are left wondering about this phenomenon for many other people. What if we were to think about people's lives more as works of art? Anyone's life, not just the great artists among us. Is there a sense in which many of our loved ones can achieve a kind of greatness in story after they are dead, as we remember them in a way that is not possible while we are caught up with the details of living? If so, then perhaps the process of distilling and refining that takes place in the course of remembering can turn the ordinary and familiar events of life into acts of greatness. Perhaps. We can achieve this aesthetic appreciation of the life of our loved ones more fully when we are able to let the dross of life drain away.

Aesthetic appreciation makes a difference to our living. It refines our sense of taste for life and teaches us moral lessons. It inspires us to take up acts of courage and warns us of dangers. It connects us with great purposes and with our shared humanity. It speaks to us of the cultural richness of particular times and places and it establishes connections across difference. So too, we suspect, do remembering conversations. When conducted with these possibilities in mind, they have a poetic purpose that is far greater in scope than simple reminiscing. They serve, as Bakhtin (1981) again says about remembering, "the future memory of a past" (p. 19). And yet they are based in the simple human pastime of telling stories.

A colleague of ours, Sharon Cottor, is fond of saying, "It is never too late to have a happy childhood." This is a counter-statement to the many deterministic theories that abound about childhood trauma. It suggests that there is nothing essential about any particular human experience. The meaning that we construct about the event has more to do with its influence on our identity. We would like to paraphrase this statement and suggest that it is never too late to have a happy death. How we remember is more important than the material circumstances of the death. How we continue to construct relationship, even after death, is more important than any particular plot event in a relationship before death. In plain language, how we tell the story matters.

In this book, we have shared some of our own stories and stories that others have shared with us. Along the way, we have often been curious about what happens to these stories in the conversations in your head. We have hypothesized the parallel conversations that you might be having with your family members—living and dead—as well as with people whom you serve in your professional practice. Our hope is that our stories will connect with and take on extra life in your conversations.

If this happens, the thoughts inspired by our words now become communal and relational space. They are no longer just John's and Lorraine's renditions, but take on new dimensions. Their meaning is never finalized. The main reason, after all, for committing stories to text is to prolong their life and to extend the range of the conversations in which they can live. In short, to enhance their chance of being remembered.

When we teach, we are often inspired to hear of these effects. People come to our workshops with the most delightful stories of family members, who are brought to life in the room. We continue to be inspired by hearing these stories. But we must admit to some frustration with the one way direction of writer-reader relationships. There is a nagging awareness that we only know part of the story. We would like to correct some of this imbalance. Rather than missing out on the possibility of having your stories as part of our membership club, we would like to invite you to share these with us. We would welcome a two-way connection and would like to collect more stories of remembering to share with others. You are therefore invited to e-mail us with any stories that are brought to life for you in response to reading this book. You can send them to us at this Web site address: rememberingpractices.com. This is how we would like to leave off the writing of this book—with an invitation to ongoing conversation.

References

AIDS Memorial Quilt Site. (2002). http://www.aidsquilt.org.htm. 2 August 2002.

Albom, M. (1997). *Tuesdays with Morrie, an old man, a young man and the last great lesson*. New York: Doubleday.

American Psychiatric Association. (1994). *Diagnostic and statistical manual* (4th ed.). Washington: Author.

Anderson, H. (1997). *Conversation, language, and possibilities*. New York: Basic Books.

Aries, P. (1974). *Western attitudes toward death: From the middle ages to the present* (P. Ranum, Trans.). Baltimore: Johns Hopkins University Press.

Attig, T. (1996). *How we grieve: Relearning the world*. New York: Oxford University Press.

Attig, T. (2000). *The heart of grief*. New York: Oxford University Press.

Attig, T. (2001) Relearning the world: Making meaning and finding meanings. In R. Neimeyer (Ed.), *Meaning reconstruction & the experience of loss* (pp. 33- 54). Washington D.C.: American Psychological Association.

Baines, B. (2002). *Ethical wills*. Cambridge, MA: Perseus Publishing.

Bakhtin, M. (1981). *The dialogic imagination* (C. Emerson & M. Holquist, Trans.). Austin, TX: University of Texas Press.

Bakhtin, M. (1986). *Speech genres and other late essays* (M. McGee, Trans.). Austin, TX: University of Texas Press.

Bananno, G., & Kaltman, S. (1999). Toward an integrative perspective on bereavement. *Psychological Bulletin, 125*(6), 750-776.

Barkway, P. (2001). Silent Birth. In C. White (Ed.), *Working with the stories of women's lives* (pp. 61-78). Adelaide, Australia: Dulwich Centre Publications.

Benoliel, J. (1997). Death, technology, and gender in postmodern American society. In S. Strack (Ed.), *Death and the quest for meaning* (pp. 31-56). Northvale, NJ: Jason Aronson Inc.

Bertman, S. (1997). From the very first patient to the very last: Soul pain, aesthetic distance, and the training of physicians. In S. Strack (Ed.), *Death and the quest for meaning* (pp. 163-189). Northvale, NJ: Jason Aronson Inc.

Bird, L., & Drewery, W. (2000). *Human development in Aotearoa: A journey through life*. Auckland, New Zealand: McGraw-Hill.

Bowlby, J. (1969/1980). *Attachment and loss*. London: Hogarth Press.

Bornat, J. (Ed.) (1994). *Reminiscence reviewed: Perspectives, evaluations, achievements.* Bristol, PA: Open University Press.

Bruner, J. (1986). *Actual minds, possible worlds.* Cambridge, MA: Harvard University Press.

Bruner, J. (1990). *Acts of meaning.* Cambridge, MA: Harvard University Press.

Bruner, J. (1994). The "remembered" self. In U. Neisser & R. Fivush (Eds.), *The remembering self: Construction and accuracy in the self-narrative* (pp. 41-54). New York: Cambridge University Press.

Burr, V. (1995). *An introduction to social constructionism.* London: Routledge.

Byock, I. (1997). *Dying well: A prospect for growth at the end of life.* New York: Riverhead Books.

Campbell, J. (1988). *The power of myth.* New York: Doubleday.

Capps, L., & Bonanno, G. (2000). Narrating bereavement: Thematic and grammatical predictors of adjustment to loss. *Discourse Processes, 30*(1), 1-25.

Castaneda, C. (1972). *Journey to Ixtlan: The lessons of Don Juan.* New York: Simon and Schuster.

Colgrove, M., Bloomfield, H., & McWilliams, P. (1991). *How to survive the loss of a love.* Los Angeles: Prelude Press.

Connor, S. (2002). Lessons for an aging population from the hospice model. In K. Doka (Ed.), *Living with grief: Loss in later life* (pp. 131-142). Washington, D.C.: Hospice Foundation of America.

Cupitt, D. (2000). *Philosophy's own religion.* London: SCM Press.

Curry, C. (1990). *When your spouse dies: A concise & practical source of help and advice.* Notre Dame, IN: Ave Maria Press.

Dansey, H. (1977). A view of death. In J. Cowan (Ed.), *Te Ao Hurihuri: The world moves on: Aspects of Maoritanga* (pp. 129-141). Wellington, New Zealand: Hicks Smith.

Deits, B. (1988). *Life after loss.* Tucson, AZ: Fisher Books.

Denborough, D., & White, C. (2000). Living positive lives: A gathering for people living with HIV and workers in the HIV sector. *Dulwich Centre Journal, 2000*(4), 3-37.

de Saint-Exupery, A. (1943). *The little prince.* San Diego, CA: Harvest Books.

Doka, K. (2002). *Living with grief: Loss in later life.* Washington, D.C.: Hospice Foundation of America.

Drewery, W., & Winslade, J. (1997). The theoretical story of narrative therapy. In G. Monk, J. Winslade, K. Crocket, & D. Epston (Eds.), *Narrative therapy in practice: The archaeology of hope* (pp. 32-52). San Francisco: Jossey-Bass.

Edelman, H. (1985). *Motherless daughters: The legacy of loss.* Reading, MA: Addison Wesley.

Epston, D. (1993). Internalized other questioning with couples: The New Zealand version. In S. Gilligan & R. Price (Eds.), *Therapeutic conversations* (pp. 183-189). New York: W. W. Norton & Co.

Epston, D., & White, M. (1992). *Experience, contradiction, narrative and imagination.* Adelaide, Australia: Dulwich Centre Publications.

Fairclough, N. (1992). *Discourse and social change.* Cambridge, UK: Polity Press.

Foucault, M. (1972). *The order of things.* New York: Pantheon

Foucault, M. (1978). *Discipline and punish.* (A. Sheridan, Trans.). New York: Vintage Books.

Foucault, M. (1980). *Power/knowledge: Selected interviews and other writings.* New York: Pantheon Books.

Frankl, V. (1959). *Man's search for meaning.* New York: Washington Square Press.

Frankl, V. (1978). *The unheard cry for meaning.* New York: Washington Square Press.

Frantz, T., Farrell, M., & Trolley, B. (2001). Positive outcomes of losing a loved one. In R. Neimeyer (Ed.), *Meaning reconstruction & the experience of loss* (pp. 191-209). Washington, D.C.: American Psychological Association.

Freedman, J., & Combs, G. (1996). *Narrative therapy: The social construction of preferred reality.* New York: Norton.

Freud, S. (1917/1957). Mourning and melancholia. In J. Strachey (Ed.), *The standard edition of the complete psychological works of Sigmund Freud* (Vol. 14, pp. 243-258). London: Hogarth Press. (Original work published 1917.)

Freud, S. (1938). *The basic writings of Sigmund Freud* (A. Brill, Trans. & Ed.). New York: The Modern Library.

Garland, J. (1994). What splendour, it all coheres: Life-review therapy with older people. In J. Bornat (Ed.), *Reminiscence reviewed: Perspectives, evaluations, achievements* (pp. 21-31). Bristol, UK: Open University Press.

Gatenby, B. (1998). *For the rest of our lives. After the death of a child.* Auckland, New Zealand: Reed Publishing.

Geering, L. (1994). *Tomorrow's God.* Wellington, New Zealand: Bridget Williams Books.

Gergen, K. (1994). *Realities and relationships.* Cambridge, MA: Harvard University Press.

Gergen, K. (1999). *An invitation to social construction.* London: Sage.

Gergen, M. (1987). *Social ghosts: Opening inquiry on imaginal relationships.* Paper presented at the 95th Annual Convention of the APA, New York.

Hagman, G. (2001). Beyond decathexis: Toward a new psychoanalytic understanding and treatment of mourning. In R. Neimeyer (Ed.), *Meaning reconstruction & the experience of loss* (pp. 13-31). Washington, D.C.: American Psychological Association.

Hammond, S. (1996). *The thin book of appreciative inquiry.* Plano, TX: Kodiak Consulting.

Harding, R., & Dyson, M. (1981). *A book of condolences.* New York: Continuum Press.

Hedtke, L. (1999). Multiplying death, dying & grief narratives. In J. Winslade, (Ed.), *A place to stand: Proceedings of the New Zealand Association of Counsellors conference* (pp. 201-206). Hamilton, New Zealand: University of Waikato.

Hedtke, L. (2000). Dancing with death, *Gecko: A Journal of Deconstruction and Narrative Ideas in Therapeutic Practice, 2001*(2): 3-14.

Hedtke, L. (2001a). Remembering practices in the face of death. *The Forum, Association for Death Education and Counseling, 27*(2), 5-6.

Hedtke, L. (2001b). Stories of living and dying. *Gecko: A Journal of Deconstruction and Narrative Ideas in Therapeutic Practice, 2001*(1), 4-27.

Hedtke, L. (2001c). An afterlife of stories. *The Thanatology Newsletter, 7*(4), 11-12.

Hedtke, L. (2002a). Re-thinking deathbed forgiveness rituals. *The International Journal of Narrative Therapy and Community Work, 2002*(1), 14-17.

Hedtke, L. (2002b). Reconstructing the language of death and grief. *Journal of Illness, Crisis and Loss, 10*(4), 285-293.

Hockey, J. (1990). *Experiences of death: An anthropological account.* Edinburgh, UK: Edinburgh University Press.

Hoffman, L. (1981). *Foundations of family therapy.* New York: Basic Books.

Humphry, D. (1991). *Final exit, the practicalities of self-deliverance and assisted suicide for the dying.* New York: Dell.

Keen, S., & Fox-Valley, A. (1973). *Your mythic journey.* New York: G. P. Putnam's Sons.

King, M. L. (1986). *I have a dream: Writings and speeches that changed the world* (J. Washington, Ed.). New York: HarperCollins.

Kirchner, P. (1995). *Love is the link.* Burdette, NY: Larson Publications.

Klass, D. (1996). Grief in eastern culture: Japanese ancestor worship. In D. Klass, P. Silverman, & L. Nickman (Eds.), *Continuing bonds: New understandings of grief* (pp. 59-69). Philadelphia: Taylor & Francis.

Klass, D. (2001). The inner representation of the dead child in the psychic and social narratives of bereaved parents. In R. Neimeyer (Ed.), *Meaning reconstruction & the experience of loss* (pp. 77-94). Washington, D.C.: American Psychological Association.

Klass, D., Silverman, P., & Nickman, L. (Eds.). (1996). *Continuing bonds: New understandings of grief.* Philadelphia: Taylor & Francis.

Kleiman, A. (1988). *The illness narratives.* New York: Basic Books.

Kübler-Ross, E. (1969). *On death and dying.* New York: Simon & Schuster.

Kübler-Ross, E. (1991). *On life after death.* Berkeley, CA: Celestial Arts.

Lattanzi-Licht, M., & Connor, S. (1995). Care of the dying: The hospice approach. In H. Wass & R. Neimeyer (Eds.), *Dying: Facing the facts* (pp. 143-162). Washington, D.C.: Taylor & Francis.

Lynn, J., & Harrold, J. (1999). *Handbook for mortals: Guidance for people facing serious illness.* New York: Oxford University Press.

Lyotard, J. F. (1984). *The postmodern condition.* Minneapolis: University of Minnesota Press.

Madigan, S. (1997). Re-considering memory: Re-remembering lost identities back toward re-membered selves. In C. Smith & D. Nylund (Eds.), *Narrative therapies with children and adolescents* (pp. 338-355). New York: Guilford Press.

Marshall, F. (1993). *Losing a parent: A personal guide to coping with that special grief that comes with losing a parent.* Tucson, AZ: Fisher Press.

McGoldrick, M., & Gerson, R. (1985). *Genograms in family assessment.* New York: W. W. Norton.

McLean, C. (Ed.). (1995). Reclaiming our stories, reclaiming our lives. *Dulwich Centre Newsletter, 1995*(3), 1-40.

McNamee, S., & Gergen, K. (Eds.) (1999). *Relational responsibility: Resources for sustainable dialogue.* Thousand Oaks, CA: Sage Publications.

McPhelimy, L. (1997). *A checklist of life: A working book to help you live and leave this life.* Rockfall, CT: AAIP Publishing.

Middleton, D., & Edwards, D. (Eds.). (1990). *Collective remembering.* London: Sage.

Minuchin, S. (1984). *Family kaleidoscope.* Cambridge: Harvard University Press.

Mojtabai, A. (1998). *Soon: Tales from hospice.* Cambridge: Zoland Books.

Monk, G., Neylon, E., & Sinclair, S. (in press). Deconstructing homicide bereavement: An innovative approach for working with homicide survivors. *Counseling and Guidance Journal.*

Monk, G., Winslade, J, Crocket, K., & Epston, D. (Eds.). (1997). *Narrative therapy in practice: The archaeology of hope.* San Francisco: Jossey-Bass.

Myerhoff, B. (1978). *Number our days.* New York: Simon & Schuster.

Myerhoff, B. (1982). Life history among the elderly: Performance, visibility and remembering. In J. Ruby (Ed.), *A crack in the mirror: Reflexive perspectives in anthropology* (pp. 99-117). Philadelphia: University of Pennsylvania Press.

Myerhoff, B. (1986). Life not death in Venice. In V. Turner & E. Bruner (Eds.), *The anthropology of experience* (pp. 261-286). Chicago: The University of Illinois Press.

Nadeau, J. (2001). Family construction of meaning. In R. Neimeyer (Ed.), *Meaning reconstruction & the experience of loss* (pp. 95-111). Washington D.C.: American Psychological Association.

Nadeau, J. (2002). Counseling later life families. In K. Doka (Ed.), *Living with grief: Loss in later life* (pp. 314-327). Washington, D.C.: Hospice Foundation of America.

National Hospice Organization. (1999). *Hospice Fact Sheet.* Web site information: www.nhpco.org (November 10, 2001).

National Hospice Organization (1997). *About grief.* Arlington, VA: NHO.

Neimeyer, R. (1998). *Lessons of loss: A guide to coping.* New York: McGraw Hill.

Neimeyer, R. (2000). Narrative disruptions in the construction of the self. In R. Neimeyer & J. Raskin (Eds.), *Constructions of disorder: Meaning-making frameworks for psychotherapy* (pp. 207-242). Washington, D.C.: American Psychological Association.

Neimeyer, R. (2001). The language of loss: Grief therapy as a process of meaning reconstruction. In R. Neimeyer (Ed.), *Meaning reconstruction & the experience of loss* (pp. 261-292). Washington, D.C.: American Psychological Association.

Neimeyer, R. (2002). Making sense of loss. In K. Doka (Ed.), *Living with grief: Loss in later life* (pp. 295-311). Washington, D.C.: Hospice Foundation of America.

Ngata, P. (1987). Death, dying and grief: A Maori perspective. In *Undiscovered country: Customs of the cultural and ethnic groups of New Zealand concerning death and dying* (pp. 5-14). Wellington, New Zealand: Department of Health.

Nuland, S. (1993). *How we die: Reflections on life's final chapter.* New York: Random House.

Obershaw, R. (1992). *Cry until you laugh.* Minneapolis: Fairview Press.

Paré, D. (1996). Culture and meaning: Expanding the metaphorical repertoire of family therapy. *Family Process, 35*(1), 21-42.

Parker, I. (1992). *Discourse dynamics: Critical analysis for social and individual psychology.* London: Routledge.

Pennebaker, J. (2000). The effects of traumatic disclosure on physical and mental health: The values of writing and talking about upsetting events. In J. Violanti & D. Paton et al. (Eds.), *Posttraumatic stress intervention: Challenges, issues, and perspectives* (pp. 97-114). Springfield, IL: Charles C. Thomas Publisher.

Richards, T. A. (2001). Spiritual resources following a partner's death from AIDS. In Neimeyer, R. (Ed.), *Meaning reconstruction & the experience of loss.* Washington, D.C.: American Psychological Association.

Rosenblatt, P. (1996). Grief that does not end. In D. Klass, P. Silverman, & L. Nickman (Eds.), *Continuing bonds: New understandings of grief* (pp. 45-48). Philadelphia: Taylor & Francis.

Sampson, E. (1993). *Celebrating the other: A dialogic account of human nature.* Boulder, CO: Westview Press.

Sarbin, T. (Ed.) (1986). *Narrative psychology: The storied nature of human conduct.* New York: Praeger.

Saunders, C. (1963). The treatment of intractable pain in terminal cancer. *Proceedings of the Royal Society of Medicine, 56,* 195-197.

Saunders, C. (2001). The evolution of palliative care. *Journal of the Royal Society of Medicine, 94*(9), 430-434.

Shapiro, E. R. (1994). *Grief as a family process.* New York: Guilford Press.

Shuchter, S. R. (1986). *Dimensions of grief: Adjusting to the death of a spouse.* San Francisco: Jossey-Bass.

Seidman, P. (Ed.). (1994). *The postmodern turn: New perspectives on social theory.* New York: Cambridge University Press.

Silverman, P., & Klass, D. (1996). Introduction: What's the problem? In D. Klass, P. Silverman, & L. Nickman (Eds.), *Continuing bonds: New understandings of grief* (pp. 3-27). Philadelphia: Taylor & Francis.

Silverman, P., & Nickman, L. (1996). Children's construction of their dead parents. In D. Klass, P. Silverman, & L. Nickman (Eds.), *Continuing bonds: New understandings of grief* (pp. 73-86). Philadelphia: Taylor & Francis.

Smith, P., & Behan, C. (2002). *Living conversations.* Portland: Fresh Press.

St. Christopher's hospice Web site (Feb. 2002). http/www.stchristophers.org.uk

Stroebe, M., Gergen, M., Gergen, K., & Stroebe, W. (1996). Broken hearts or broken bonds? In D. Klass, P. Silverman, & L. Nickman (Eds.), *Continuing bonds: New understands of grief* (pp. 31-44). Philadelphia: Taylor & Francis.

Stroebe, M., & Schut, H. (2001). Meaning making in the dual process model of coping with bereavement. In R. Neimeyer (Ed.), *Meaning reconstruction & the experience of loss* (pp. 55-73). Washington, D.C.: American Psychological Association.

Thanatology Newsletter (2002). *8*(1).

Thurber, J. (1931). *The Thurber carnival.* New York: Harper & Brothers.

Tiller, E. (2002). Rituals and stories: Creative approaches to loss in later life. In K. Doka (Ed.), *Living with grief: Loss in later life* (pp. 337-350). Washington, D.C.: Hospice Foundation of America.

Tomm, K. (1996). *Internalized other questioning: Workshop presentation.* Hamilton, New Zealand: University of Waikato.

Tomm, K., Hoyt, M., & Madigan, S. (1998). Honoring our internalized others and the ethics of caring: A conversation with Karl Tomm. In M. Hoyt (Ed.), *The handbook of constructive therapies* (pp. 198-218). San Francisco: Jossey-Bass.

Turner, V. (1986). Dewey, Dilthey, and drama: An essay in the anthropology of experience. In V. Turner & E. Bruner (Eds.), *The anthropology of experience.* Urbana: The University of Chicago Press.

van Gennep, A. (1960). *The rite of passage.* Chicago: Chicago University Press.

Vickio, C. (1999). Together in spirit: Keeping our relationships alive when loved ones die. *Death Studies, 23*(2), 161-175.

Waldegrave, J. (1999). Towards "settled stories": Working with children when a child or parent dies in a family. In A. Morgan (Ed.), *Once upon a time . . . Narrative therapy with children and their families* (pp. 173-191). Adelaide, Australia: Dulwich Centre Publications.

Wass, H., & Neimeyer, R. (Eds.). (1995). *Dying: Facing the facts.* Washington, D.C.: Taylor & Francis.

Weingarten, K. (2000). Witnessing, wonder and hope. *Family Process, 39*(4), 389-402.

White, M. (1989). Saying hullo again. In M. White, *Selected papers.* Adelaide, Australia: Dulwich Centre Publications.

White, M. (1995). *Re-Authoring lives: Interviews & essays.* Adelaide, Australia: Dulwich Centre Publications.

White, M. (1997). *Narratives of therapists' lives.* Adelaide, Australia: Dulwich Centre Publications.

White, M. (2001). Folk psychology and narrative practice. *Dulwich Centre Journal, 2001*(2), 3-37.

White, M., & Epston, D. (1990). *Narrative means to therapeutic ends.* Adelaide, Australia: Dulwich Centre Publications.

Wingard, B., & Lester, J. (2001). *Telling our stories in ways that make us stronger.* Adelaide, Australia: Dulwich Centre Publications.

Winslade, J., & Monk, G. (2000). *Narrative mediation: A new approach to conflict resolution.* San Francisco: Jossey-Bass.

Wittgenstein, L. (1958). *Philosophical investigations.* Oxford, UK: Blackwell.

Worden, J. W. (1982/1991). *Grief counseling and grief therapy: A handbook for the mental health practitioner* (2nd ed.). New York: Springer.

Zimmerman, J., & Dickerson, V. (1996). *If problems talked: Narrative therapy in action.* New York: Guilford.

Index